50/2000

# PATTERNS THAT CONNECT

The Wildlife Intaglio Etchings of Anne London and John Ballou

Text and Poetry by Bruce C. Eriksen, with additional Poetry by John Ballou

A Wind Dance Publication

Additional copies of this
volume may be ordered from,
Wind Dance Publications
113 Rice Lane,
Larkspur, CA. 94939

Typeset by Jana Janus, San Francisco, California.
Printed by McNaughten & Gunn Lithographers,
Ann Arbor, Michigan.
Printed on Warrenflo acid-free paper.



A WIND DANCE PUBLICATION

ISBN 0-932473-25-3

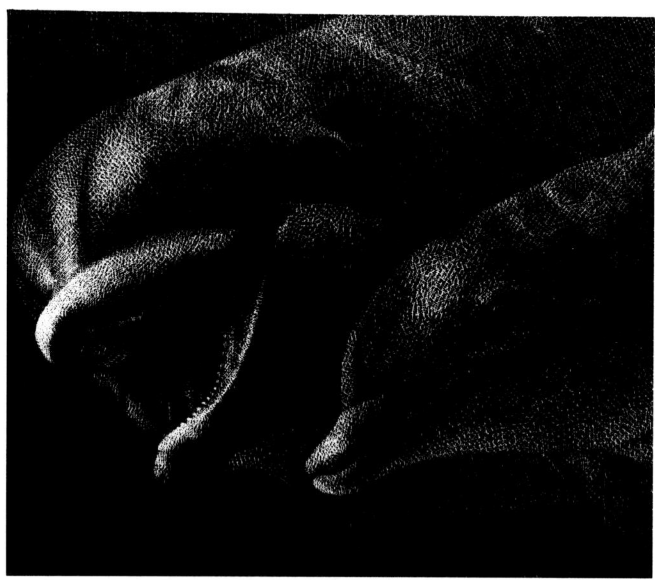

# PATTERNS THAT CONNECT

When the whale sounds
We take a breath of air.
When the dolphin leaps
Our souls also soar.
When the raven crows
We too speak,
And when the wolf hunts
We sense the reason to persist.
These are the patterns that connect us
To the pulse of life.

*Bruce C. Eriksen*

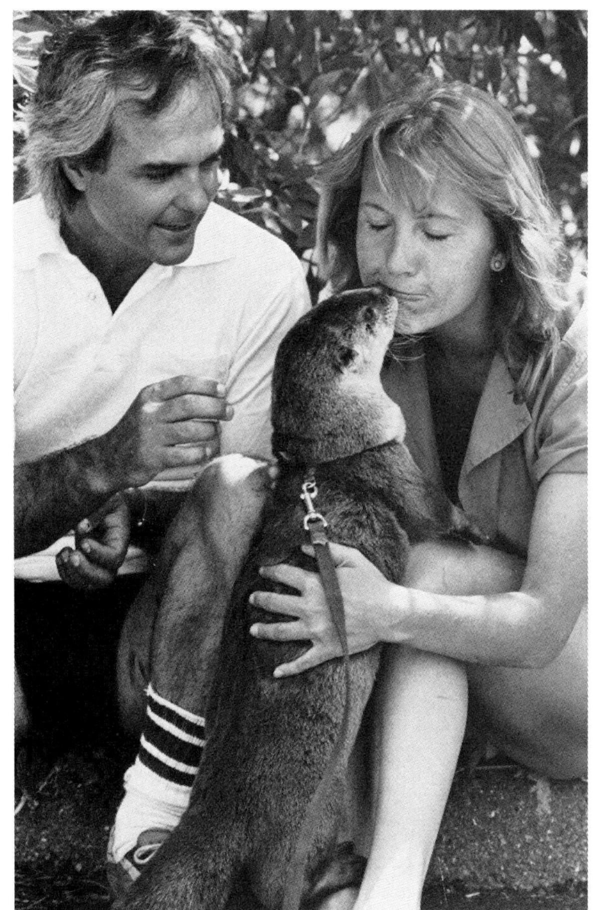

Photo by Adriana Muñoz

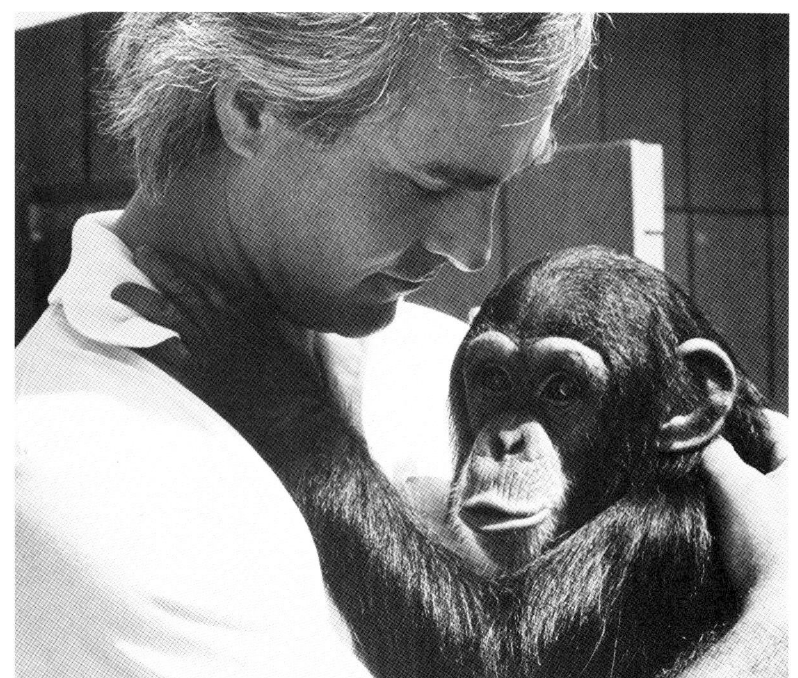

Photo by Adriana Muñoz

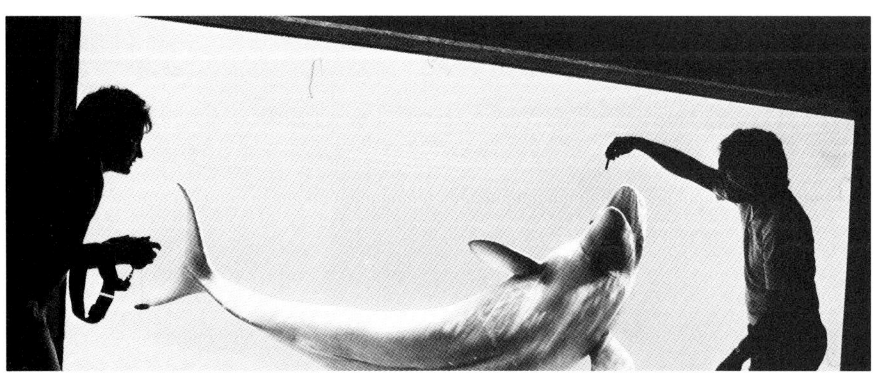

Photo by Tom Reese

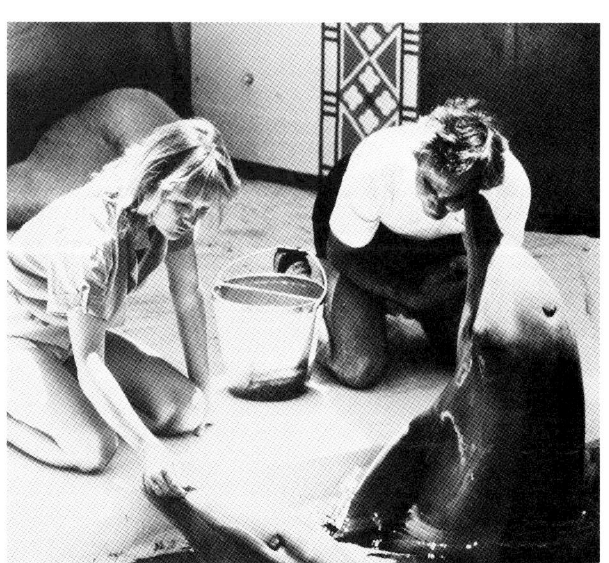

Photo by Adriana Muñoz

# *Foreword*

Our scientists, poets, and artists all have different ways of communicating about what they observe and how they feel about the world around them. We all offer representations, or models, in trying to convey our perceptions to others. John Ballou and Anne London have a very special way of seeing other animals and of communicating their perceptions and feelings about them through exquisite and haunting intaglio etchings. The images they create represent their incredible and sensitive vision for the beauty and connection that exist throughout the animal world. Their love of wildlife and their strong commitment to its preservation are clearly visible and radiated in their etchings. The intricately woven lines reveal forms and patterns that coalesce into three-dimensional living, feeling creatures. Their eyes gaze out at us from their two-dimensional world. The patterns begin to connect.

Diana Reiss, Ph.D.
*Head of Project Circe,*
Marine World Africa U.S.A.,
Dolphin Communication Studies
*Instructor of Communications,*
San Francisco State University

# *Table of Contents*

# *Dedication*

We dedicate this book to the men and women who, individually, in groups, and in organizations are daily on the forefront, fighting for the preservation of the world's wild life.

We would also like to give special mention to Diana Reiss, Ph.D., Bruce Silverman, and Marine World Africa, USA for their cooperation in many of the studies necessary for this book.

The author would like to give a special thanks to writer, teacher, and editor Betty Hodson for her encouragement and invaluable suggestions towards the completion of this book. Also, thank you Jim Brandon and Nancy Chien-Eriksen for your support and attention to detail, and Jana Janus for your hard work and enthusiastic contribution to the design and typesetting of this book.

# Introduction

Could you imagine a world without music, literature, films, dance, painting and sculpture? It would be an empty place. The same would be true in a world without eagles, seals, polar bears, whales, dolphins, wolves, leopards and other wild creatures. Yet most of us take their existence for granted and forget how greatly they enrich the texture of our lives. The loss of any species is irretrievable and drastically reduces the quality of our coexistence. When our connections to evolution are severed, we become more and more removed from the fabric of Nature. Life begins to lose its resonance, becoming more hollow.

Most of us have become so absorbed in our self-created technology that we have forgotten the delicate balance that our planet depends upon. We are the most preoccupied species on earth—obsessed with the promise of the future and ignoring the gifts of the past. We forget to look around and acknowledge the treasures we already have. Sometimes we must be reminded to appreciate our miraculous co-inhabitants, which no amount of high technology could recreate. Fortunately not everyone remains apathetic.

***To allow these creatures to exist is to declare a celebration of life itself.***

To educate as well as to inspire, John Ballou and Anne London offer these meticulous renderings of the patterns they see in Nature. They have found a way to communicate those patterns in a vision which inspires. Within their vision we may encounter the inherent value in these beloved creatures; we may experience our kinship with them.

Numerous other publications not only offer technical details and statistical data, they also present valid and excellent arguments for the preservation of endangered species. This book is meant to complement those efforts with an artist's view of some of the species which need our protection. With art and poetic prose we appeal directly to the aesthetic sensibility which exists in all of us. If that part is dormant in some of us, perhaps it will be awakened by seeing these wonderful creatures from within their habitat. This natural knowing about the balance of Nature, in the form of art, can bypass intellectual reasoning and touch us most directly in our hearts, where our true motivation lies.

John and Anne see their collaboration in this book as an opportunity to help awaken active concern for the preservation of our vanishing resources. They want these marvels of Nature to continue to thrive in the wild as well as in our imaginations. The words that I have chosen to accompany their art are a complement to what the art itself says best, as that art, in turn, is meant to complement Nature.

Perceiving this bounty is the first step towards a realization that there is more to living than mere survival. To allow these creatures to continue to exist is to declare a celebration of life itself.

*Bruce C. Eriksen*

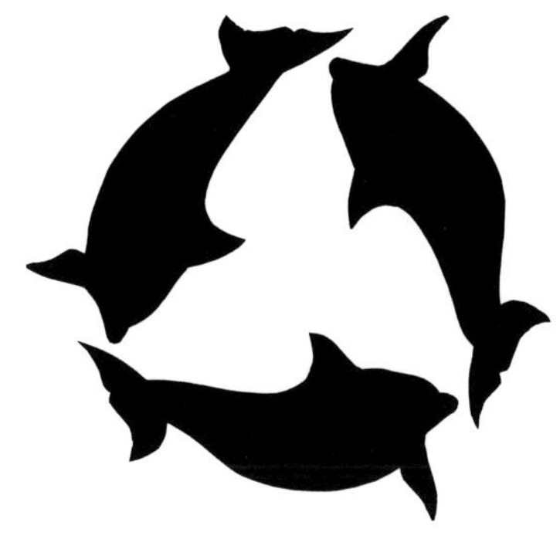

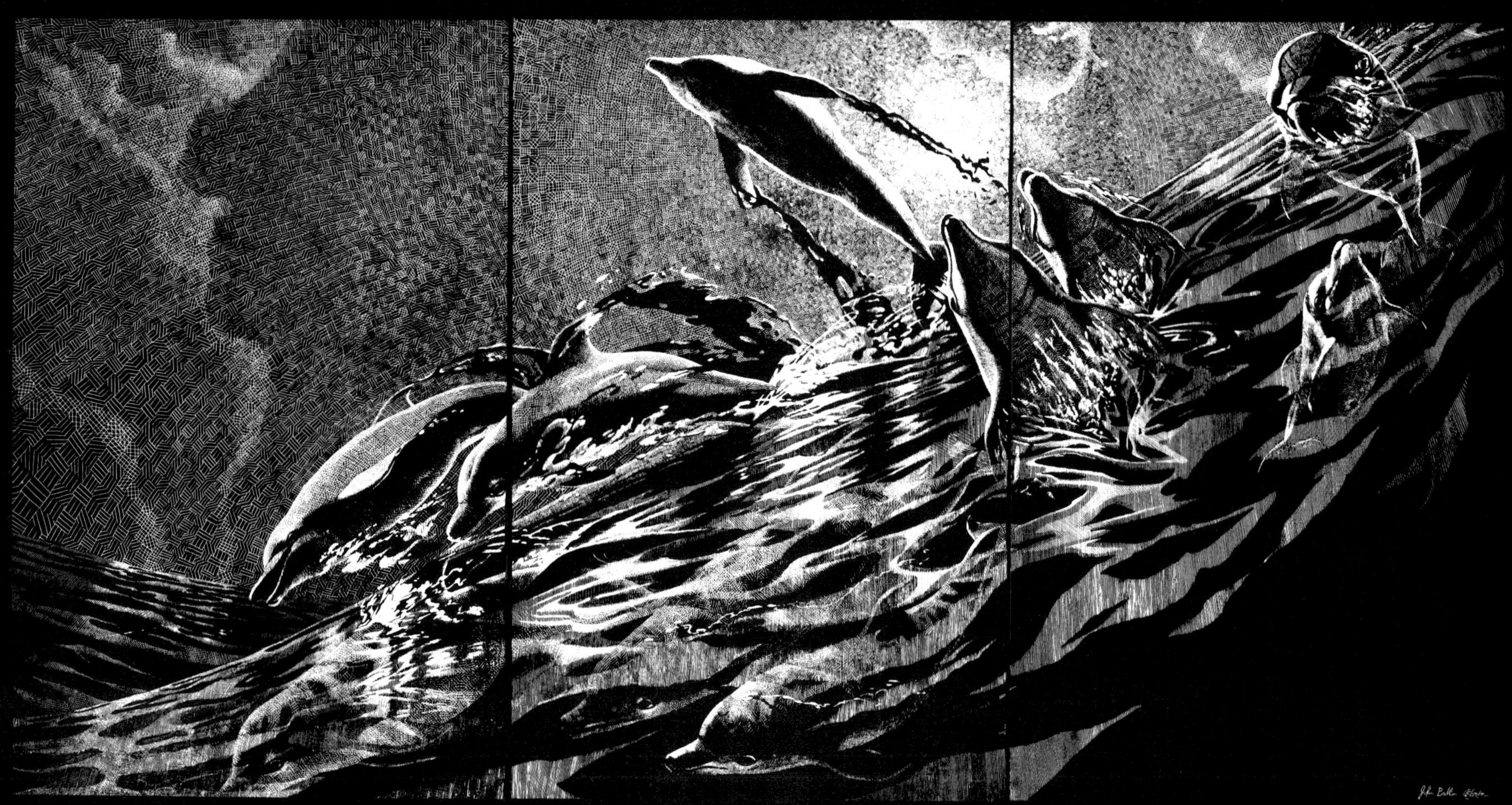

# *JOIE DE VIVRE*

Jump up my friends;
Throw your bodies high.
Fall back to a wet embrace,
To jump again,
Higher, faster, further.
Sing for living;
Dance on, my friends.
Dream of fishes and chases,
Of deep sea caverns,
Of sea foam chasing waves.
Dance on my friends;
Dance upon the waters.

*John Ballou*

# PRELUDE

Two companions
Glide
In the gentle current
And filtered sunlight
In recess
From their lighthearted
dance.

The motion
Of the undulating current
Gently wraps them
In the blanket
Of their emotion.

Their mutual rhythm
Beats...
Lazily,
Tenderly,
In the cool depths
Of hydro-space.

*Bruce C. Eriksen*

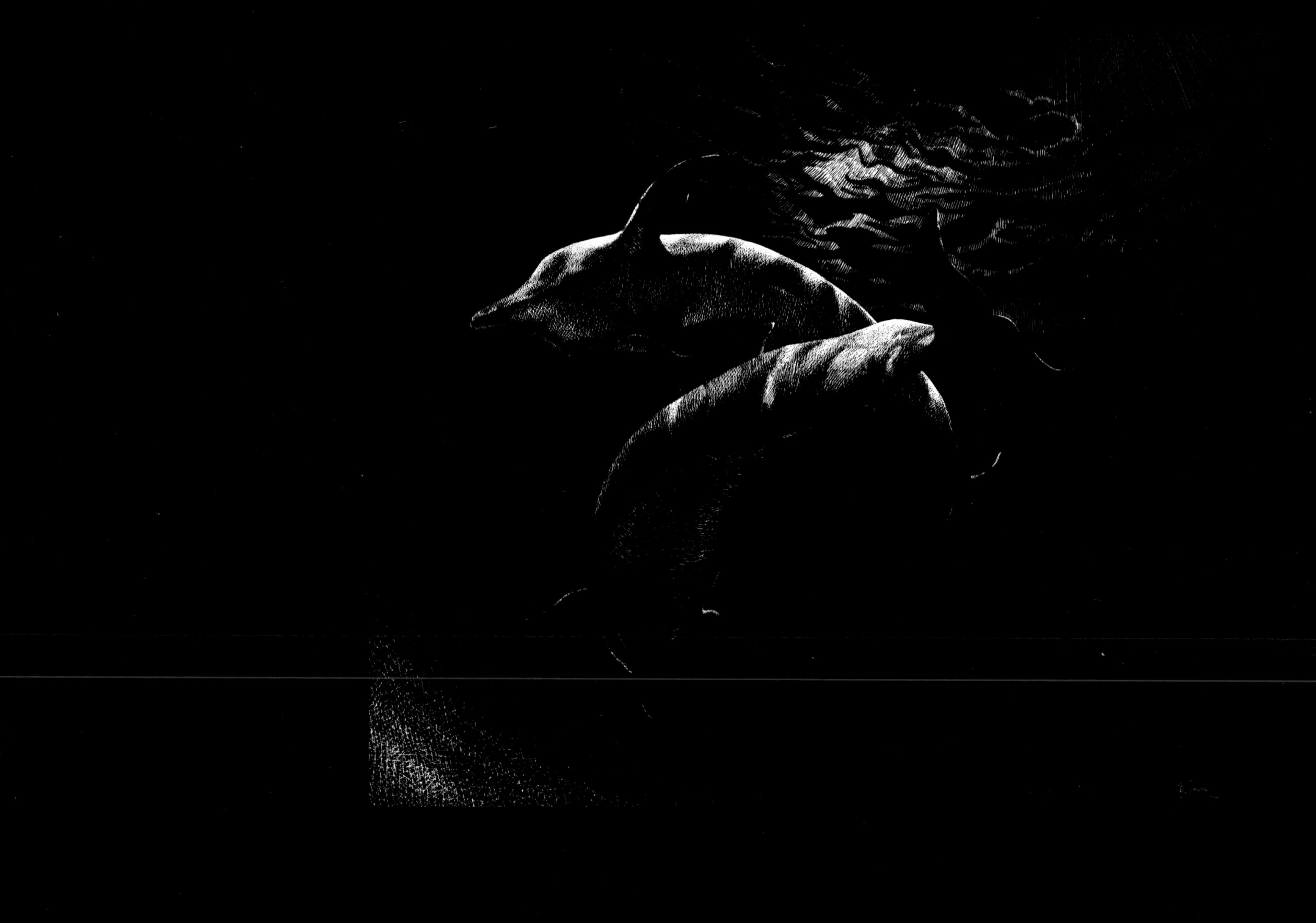

# TERRY AND PANAMA

Suspended
In the sustenance
Of their watery womb
They nourish one another
With the mingling
Of their heart beats.

They drift
The restless expanse
Which ebbs and flows
Between the tropic balm
And the arctic cold.

To live their life,
Bathing,
In the teeming caldron
From which life sprang
Is their destiny.

*Bruce C. Eriksen*

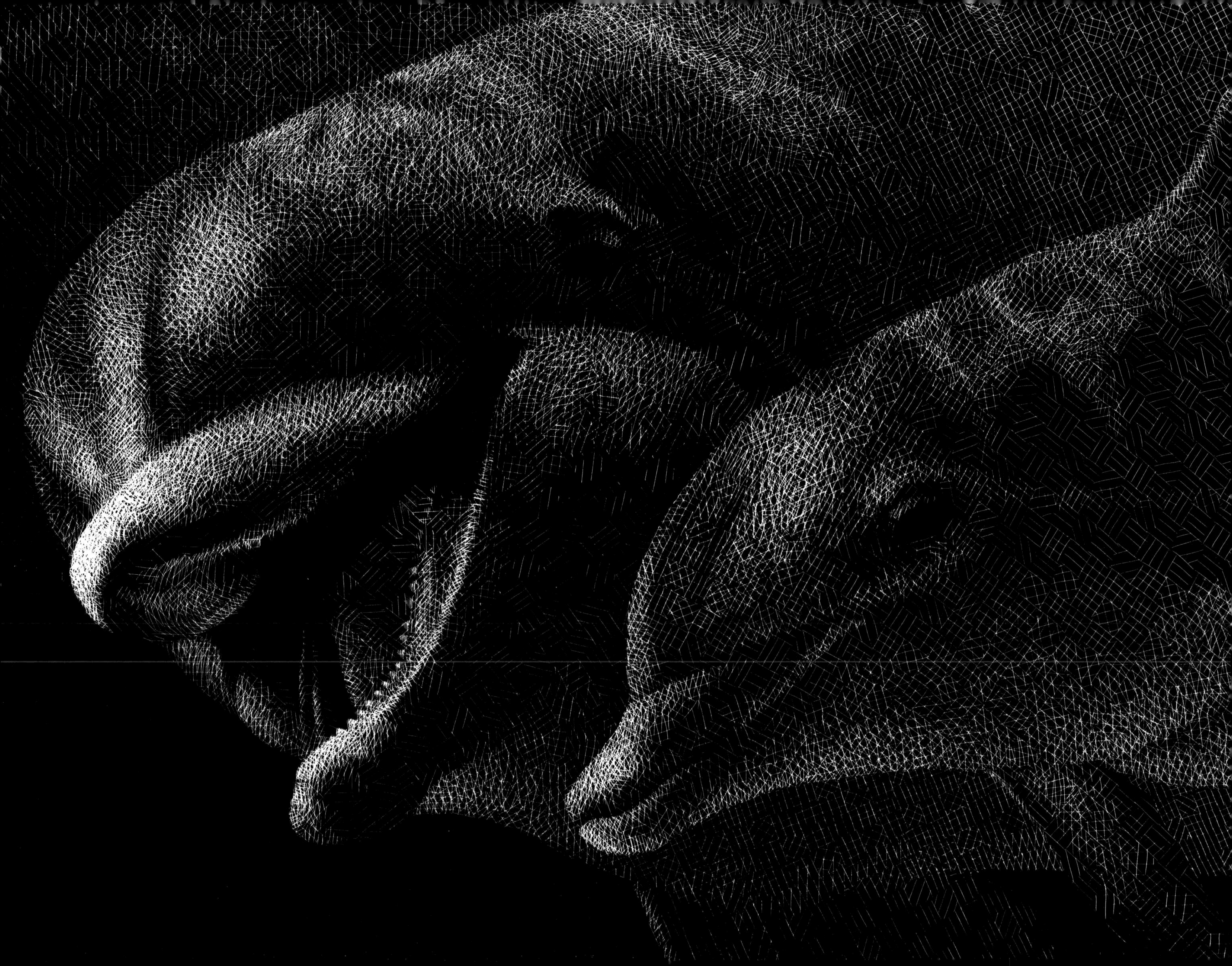

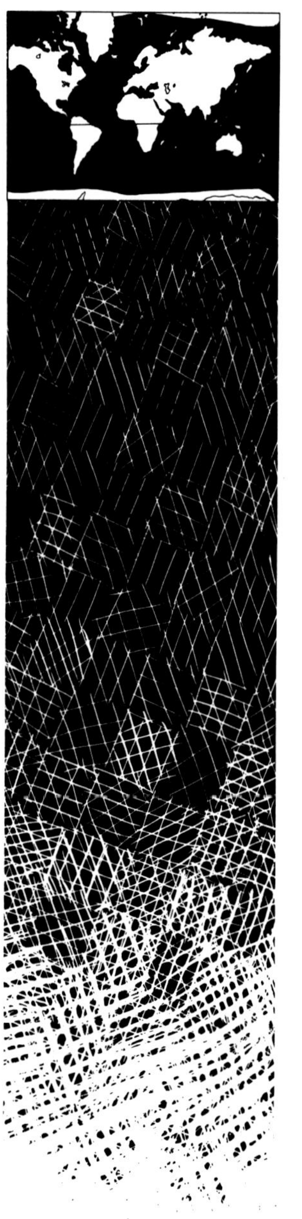

## *The Geographical Distribution of the Bottlenose Dolphin*

Bottlenose dolphins are found in almost all habitats except the very high latitudes. They are most common in the Pacific from as far north as Japan and Southern California to as far south as Australia and Chile. They are found in the Atlantic from Nova Scotia and Norway to the tip of South Africa. They are also quite common in the Mediterranean Sea and the Indian Ocean. Dolphins often enter harbors, bays, estuaries and river mouths, traveling as far inland as several miles. Usually they travel in the oceans in groups of five to twenty-five. The dolphins tend to stay in the same limited offshore neighborhood within a range of twenty miles.

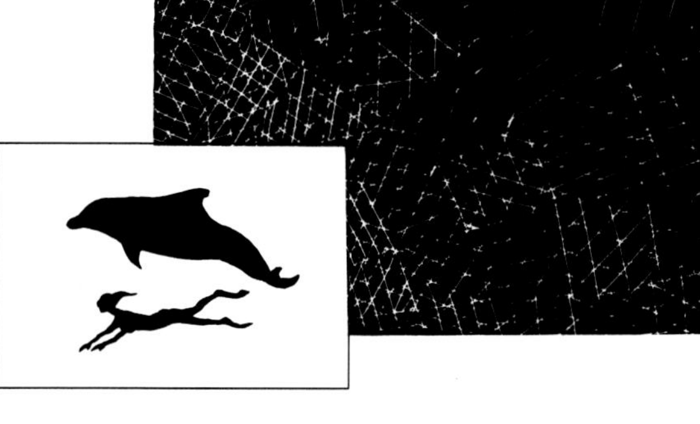

# BOTTLENOSE DOLPHINS

*(Tursiop Truncatus)*

Illustrated in this chapter is Terry who gave birth to her calf, Panama, in the summer of '83 at Marine World Africa U.S.A. in California. The close nurturing relationship of dolphins to their offspring is similar to humans. In the wild, other female dolphins appoint themselves midwives. At birth they make sure that the newborn is able to swim to the surface for air while the mother recovers, and they remain protective, especially against sharks. The bottlenose dolphin suckles under water and must return to the surface to breath every half minute. It takes five months or longer before the calf attempts to swallow solid food, so it must stay close to its mother until weaned.

Their unique and well developed sonar system allows for the receiving and focusing of acoustic signals to obtain an accurate picture of the kind and location of fast moving prey. Dolphins have a definite preference for squid, though they also feed on a wide variety of other invertebrates and fish. This preference may explain why they are often found with herds of squid-eating pilot whales. Well known as bow riders in the wake of moving vessels, they will go great distances out of their way to frolic in the pressure waves created by large whales and boats.

Dolphins are often killed for food. The Turkish alone were catching 176,000 per year in the early 1970's. Many nations including the United States and the Soviet Union have taken steps to limit their capture, but a great many are still taken directly or incidentally in beach trammel-net and gill-net fishing.

Other less obvious threats to dolphins are the offshore pollution by toxic chemicals and acoustic disturbances from boats. This could explain recent declines in population in the North Sea and English Channel and could be affecting populations in the Mediterranean and off the coast of Southern California. Also, direct competition for particular fish species may be a potential threat as man turns increasingly towards the sea as a food source. Occasionally groups of dolphins have been found stranded upon beaches and rocks, perhaps because of parasitic infections, underwater disturbances of the magnetic or artificial type, or disorientation when out of its usual hunting region.

The bottlenose dolphins are among the most sociable and entertaining of the sea mammals. Because of their remarkable intelligence they are often featured in films, shows, and performances at aquariums. A certain amount of communication and language has developed between our species and the dolphins. Because their communication is so complex, many researchers speculate that, in their own way, dolphins and their relatives are at least as intelligent as we are. It is yet to be seen whether or not their unique relationship with us will prove to be their salvation or ruin. We must decide whether or not to treat them as pets, as a commodity, or as gentle neighbors.

## ICE CAVERNS

They tumble
In a ballet
Through the cool chambers
Of a frozen cathedral,

A dance
Reserved for the few
Who, on captured breath,
Find themselves
On a stage
Of icy architecture.

Weightlessly
They undulate
Among the soft reflections
Of alabaster light
Which fades
Into the darkness
Of cavernous shadows.

*Bruce C. Eriksen*

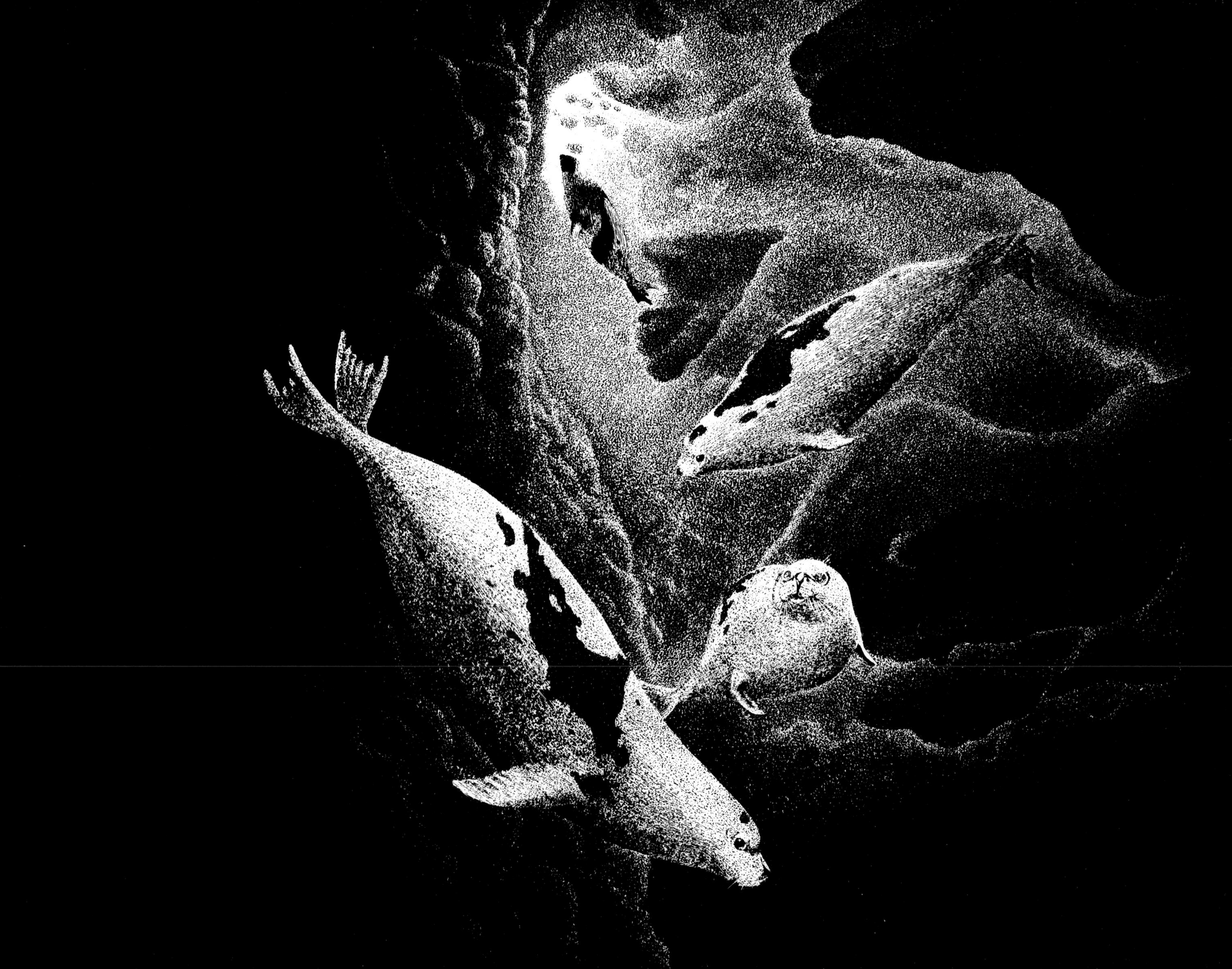

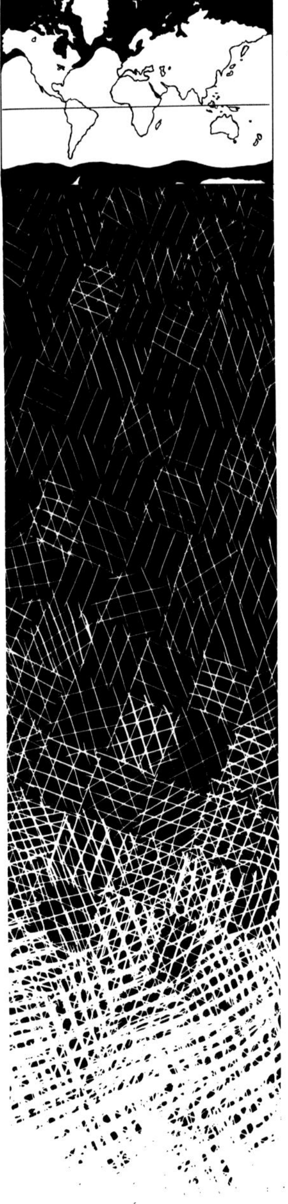

# *The Geographical Distribution of the Harp Seal*

Seals live in the coldest regions of the oceans, generally in polar, subpolar and temperate seas, land fast ice, pack ice and offshore rocks and islands. There are three main populations. These are found in the seas around Jan Mayen, Novaya Zemlya and Newfoundland. They are seen very occasionally between Scotland and the Shetland Islands.

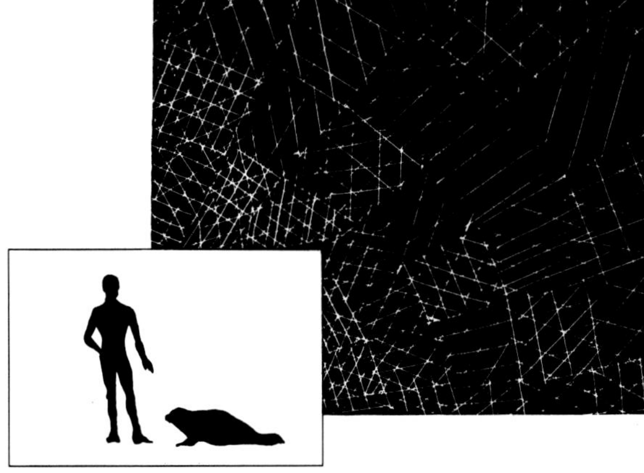

# HARP SEAL

*(Phoca groenlandica)*

These earless seals are highly efficient swimmers who are able to dive hundreds of feet for durations of twenty minutes or longer. Because their webbed hind flippers are permanently turned backwards they must move on land by body contractions and sliding. In the sea, however, they swim gracefully by using their fins combined with powerful sideways movements of their hind quarters.

The pups of the ice breeding harp seal rapidly increase in size up to three-and-a-half-fold during lactation, a period of eight to ten weeks. This transfer of the fat content of the mother to the pup is crucial to its survival in the harsh arctic climate. The "whitecoat" weaned pups are called "beaters" by the sealers. For four to six weeks after they are weaned they remain on the ice until hunger compells them to enter the water and feed mostly on soft food such as mollusks. It is during this stage that they are most helpless and valuable to hunters.

The harp seal is shy on land. Migrating herds have been recorded to gather in conglomerations of five hundred or more on ice packs. If approached near their haul out area, they will dive in mass back into the water where they are better able to protect themselves. Because of their vulnerability on land they need protection from human disturbance. The plight of the helpless harp seal pups has been dramatized by the media as of late. Still the pups are routinely slaughtered mercilessly in the initial stage of life when they are defenseless and easy prey by those who seek their fluffy white fur. Civilization is now learning about the brutality that is being perpetrated in order to make fur coats.

The European Economic Community, the E.C.C., in response to public demand led by groups such as Greenpeace, declared a ban on the importation of whitecoat pelts into their countries in 1983. As a result the seal hunt fell from 170,000 in 1982 to 56,000 in 1983, because the market for their pelts had diminished. The ban has been renewed until 1989, but not indefinitely as champions of the seal would like. The Canadian and Norwegian fishing and sealing industries continue to lobby for a lift of the ban. They claim that an unchecked seal population damages their commercial fisheries. Protesting environmentalists insist that there is no reliable evidence which supports the claim. The Norwegian government even provides subsidies to keep the hunt going, despite the stockpile of over one million pelts which remain unsold in the G.C. Rieber & Company of Bergen warehouses. Neither Canada nor Norway has changed or lowered its sealing quotas. The E.C.C.'s victory towards the preservation of the harp seal is fragile and temporary. The fishing industry is free to resume a large scale hunt at any time. The halt of the harp seal hunt depends on persistent vigilance and continued support.

# FLUKES

The solitude
Of the endless surface
Had turned my heart
Towards thoughts of isolation...
But, then,
The ceaseless sameness
Was shattered
By an eruption
Of foamy sea.

Hurled into the air
By enormous
Wings from the sea,
A great bulk
Suspended itself
Like an unfurled flag
That reminded me
Of the vitality
Which existed below.

In the ecstasy
Of that fleeting moment
Celestial time stopped.
I knew then
I was in the wake
Of a force
Before unimaginable.

Then the mighty one
Slipped back
Into his mysterious abode,
And left me
To wonder.

*Bruce C. Eriksen*

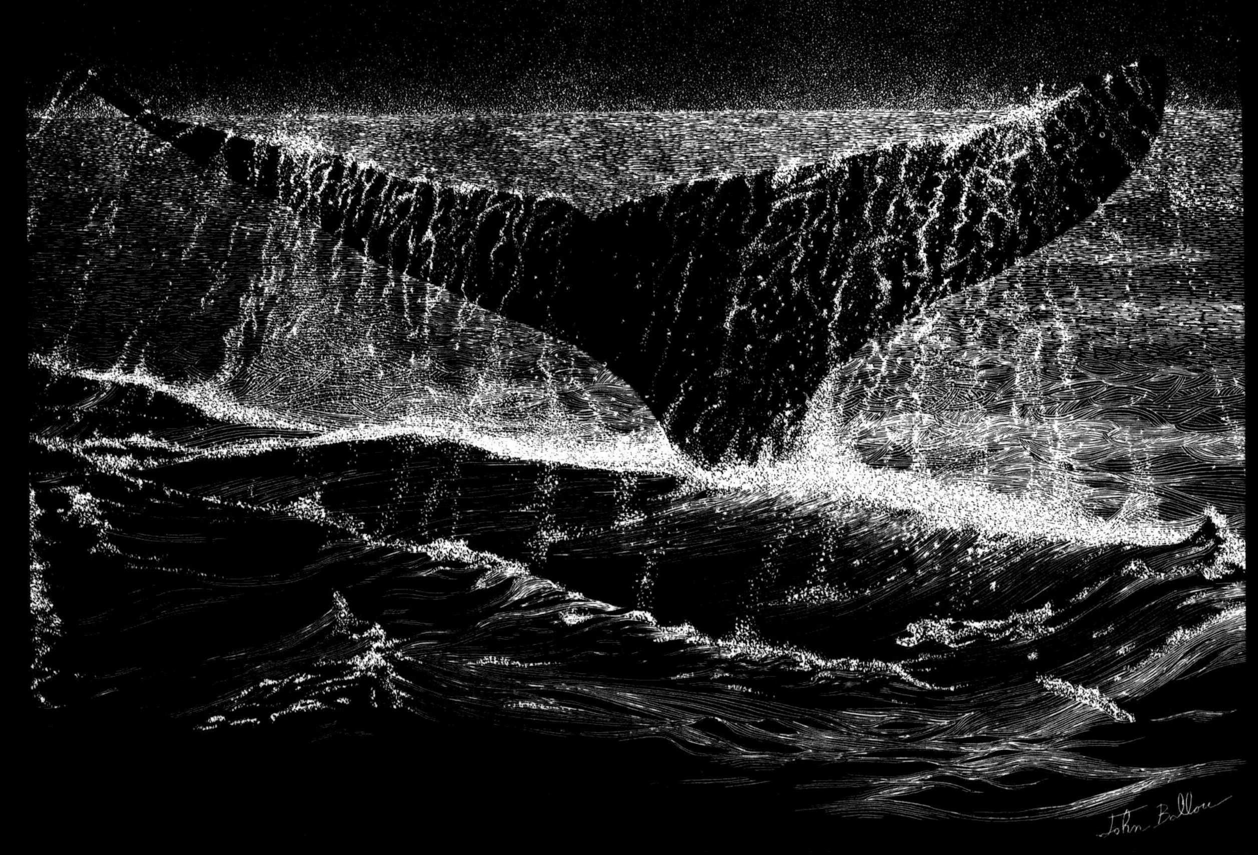


# FLUKES

Winds blow,
Storms rage,
Yet the vastness is untouched.
She lulls my body,
She pulls my spirit,
And I can but follow.

*John Ballou*

# LONG SHADOWS

Suddenly,
Across the virgin snow,
A light
Casts long shadows
That reveal alert eyes,
Surprised
By the harsh glare.

Momentarily,
A hush
Pervades the still, cold air,
As the silent ones pause
To scrutinize
The sudden intrusion.

Cautiously
They adjust,
Not yet ready to flee
The territory
That they have made
Theirs.

Abruptly
The tall ones
Have brought the day
Into the night,
And have blotted out the stars
To better see
What is at their feet.

Wisely,
A decision is made
To depart
The staring eyes
Of those
Who do not heed
Well marked boundaries.

Swiftly,
Tracks are left
On the sparkling blanket
Towards another
Less crowded hunting ground,
Where only the moon
Casts
Long shadows.

*Bruce C. Eriksen*

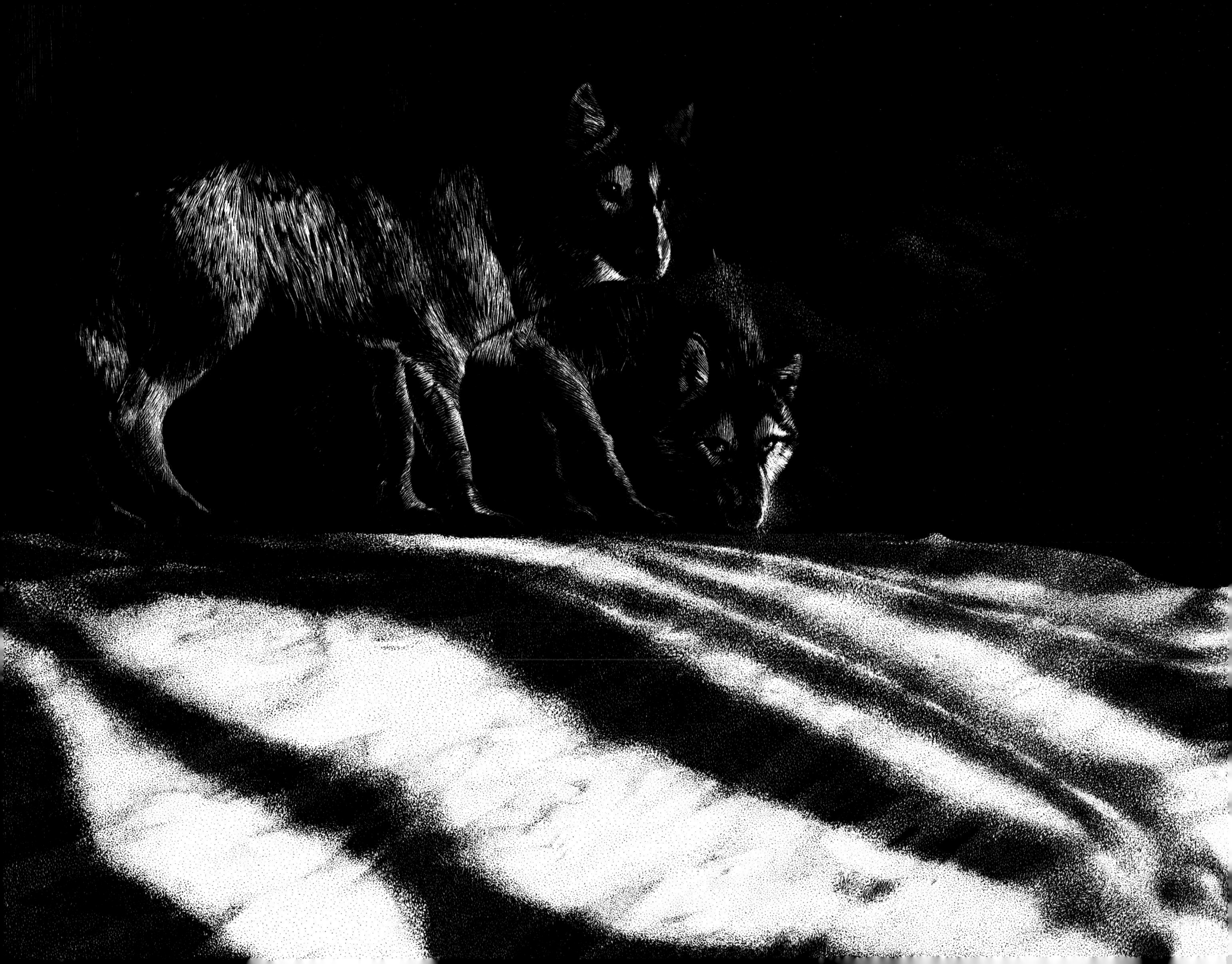

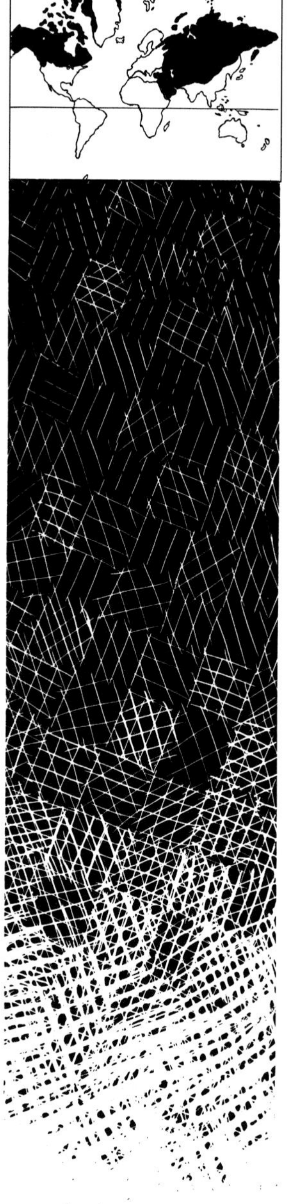

# *The Geographical Distribution of the Wolf*

Once the most widespread mammals except for man, the wolves ranged in the forests and mountains over almost all of the northern hemisphere. Now they are found in Alaska and Canada, including the arctic islands (except for the areas of Quebec, east of the St. Lawrence River, the Maritime Provinces and Newfoundland). In the lower United States they are limited to Michigan's upper peninsula, extreme northern Minnesota, Wisconsin, with packs sparsely scattered in Wyoming, Colorado, Utah, Montana, Idaho, Washington, Texas, Arizona, and New Mexico. Wolves are also found in a few large forests in Eastern Europe and some isolated mountains in Asia and the Soviet Union.

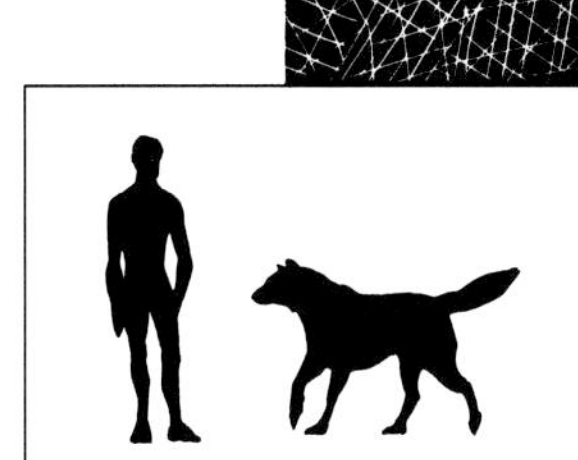

# ARCTIC WOLF

*(Canis lupis)*

In mythology and literature the wolf is often presented as a terrible, malevolent beast who will attack with a bloodthirsty nature if given the least chance. Who could forget Tchaikovsky's *Peter and the Wolf* or *The Three Little Pigs* and their adventures with the Big Bad Wolf? In real life, wolves are cooperative family members who are very selective in their hunting habits. They are shy and rarely come in contact with humans.

Family units, or packs, are led by the strongest male. All members of the pack take part in caring for the young. The litter of five to fourteen pups lives in a den for one month before briefly venturing outside. When a hunting party returns to the den from a hunt, the hungry pups nip the elders' snouts after which those elders regurgitate undigested meat for them to eat. The wolf pack's attentiveness to its young and its nurturing social behavior have given rise to folklore which abounds with tales of human children raised by wolves.

One pack's hunting territory is usually a one hundred to two hundred square mile area and overlaps the territory of other packs. Usually wolves hunt at night and use cooperative tactics to bring down large herbivores such as deer and caribou. However, their diet consist primarily of small animals, birds, fish, insects, and even berries and other fruit.

The distinctive behavior of the wolf most familiar to man is its howl. It is often performed as a part of the ritual preparatory to the hunt. After one wolf begins, the others will gather in a circle and join in the chorus. Their vocabulary is rich with barks, yaps, whines, and growls. Each inflection has its particular meaning. For instance, when one is separated from the pack it will send out short fading lonesome howls to signal its location.

Due to the encroachment of farmers, sheep herders, and cattle raisers, the wolf's habitat and populations have been greatly reduced. Because they are considered a competitor for game animals and a threat to livestock, bounties have been offered to control them. In reality, wolves seldom prey on healthy, large animals unless those animals are mired in mud or ice. In fact, they cull out the weak and infirm individuals; this ultimately benefits the survival of the species they prey upon.

Although feared in many parts of the world, attacks on people are extremely rare. Some scientific observers have even befriended them in the wild. In recent years a surge of films and studies have vividly documented the admirable traits of the wolf. Wolves are newly appreciated and their popularity among the public has increased. Unfortunately, as a result, many attempts have been made to keep them as pets. Those attempts are usually unsuccessful because the wolf has instincts for survival not appropriate to domestic life. In captivity wolves are able to fulfill only a shadow of their potential. The magnificence in wolves which humans admire can only be truly appreciated when they are observed in the natural, unfettered state they thrive in.

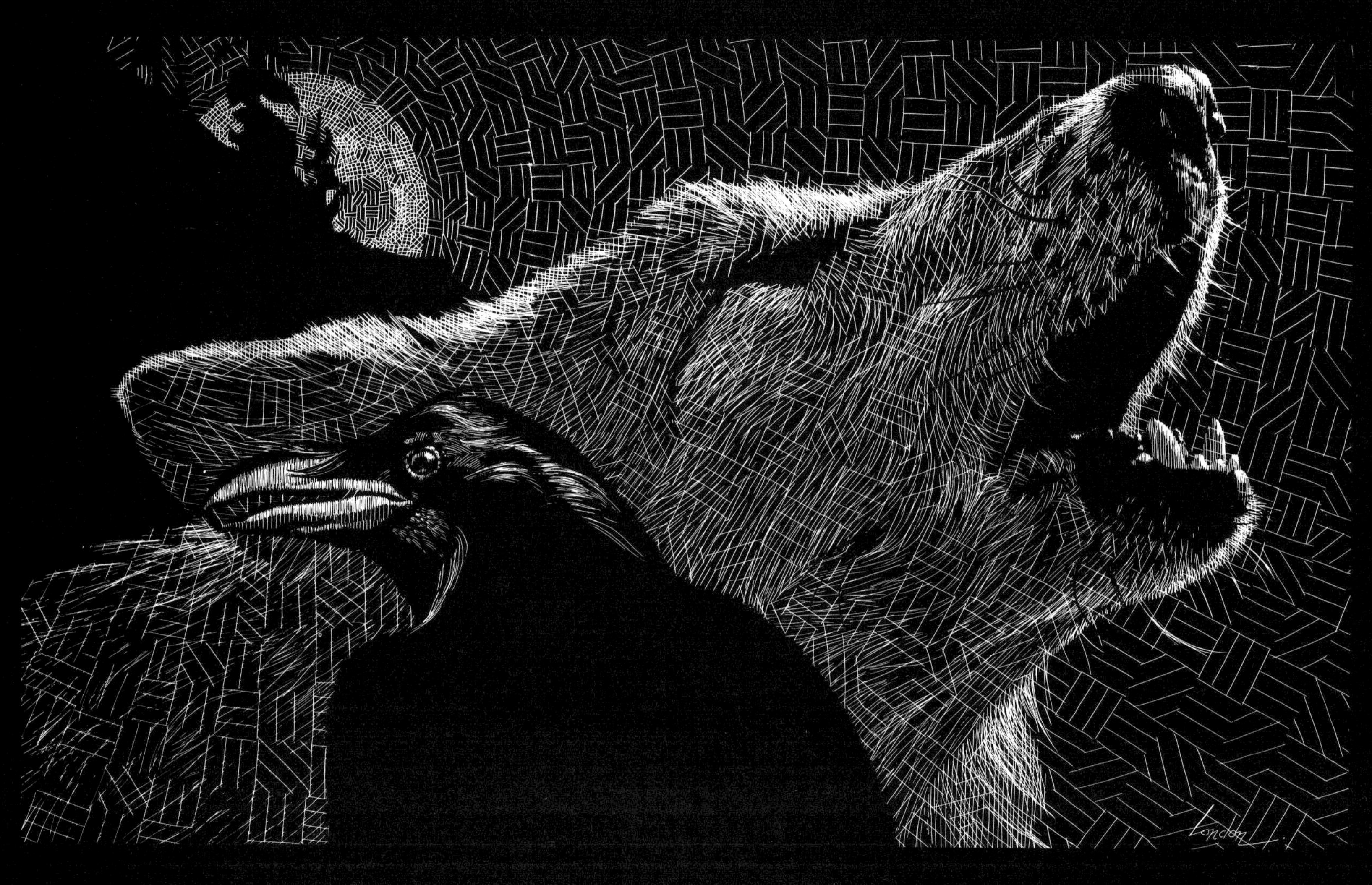
London

# THE WOLF AND THE RAVEN

Howling,
Crooning at the moon,
Your sound fills up my night.

I know you—
I know you not.
I cannot tell.

Perched on high
I feel delight.
Together tonight
We dine.

Howling,
Crooning to the moon,
Your sound fills up my night.

Up my friend,
I've prey in sight!
Hunger has set its bite.

*John Ballou*

# THE LESSON

Your mother beckons you
With your favorite treat,
Follow
Your taste
For adventure.

Put fear aside.
It is time
To trust your ability
And delay no more
On your path
To strength and wisdom.

It is your destiny
To glide
Among the seaweed strands
In an endless game
Of hide and seek.

Once away
From the secure pleasures
Of the breast,
And uncertainty is endured,
Life will be your own
To sustain and unfold.

Be brave little one.
Follow;
Begin your swim
Through the untried world
Of plenty.

*Bruce C. Eriksen*

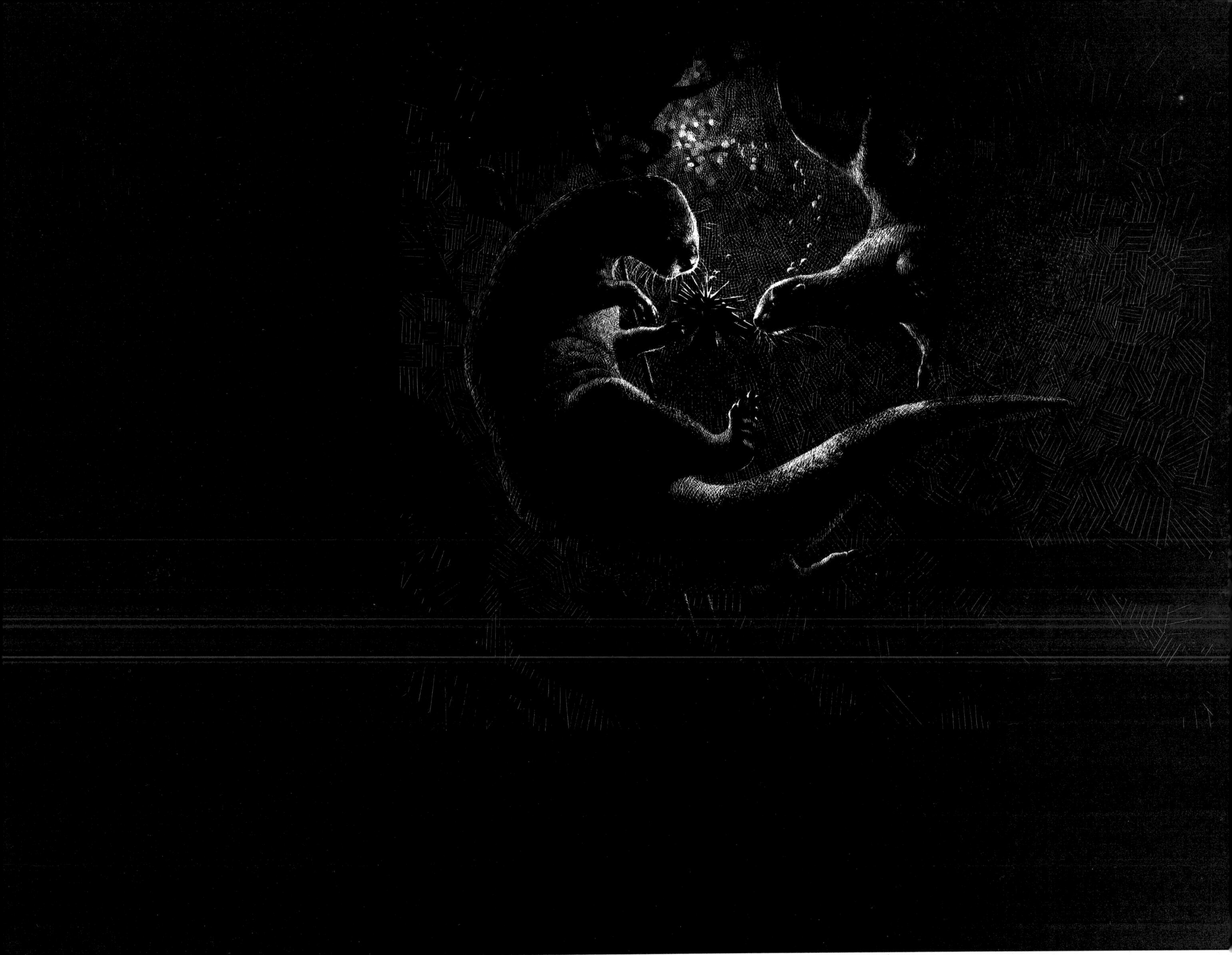

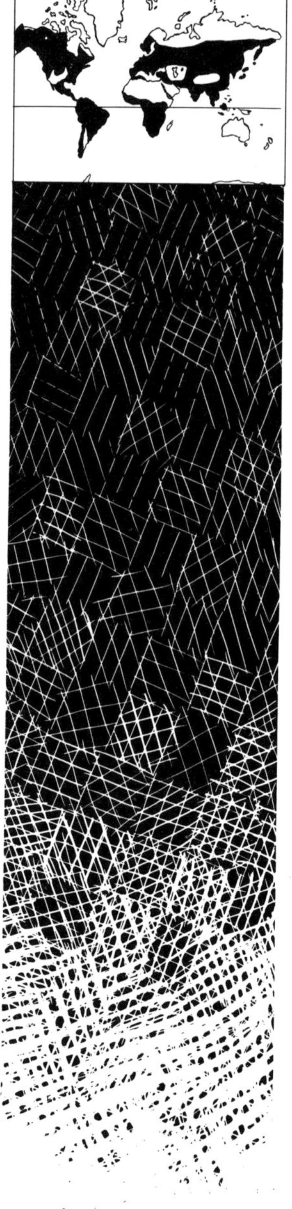

# *The Geographical Distribution of the Sea Otter*

The sea otter was once thought to be extinct. It used to be found along the coast and off shore islands from southern California to the central Bering Sea, Commander and Kurite Islands, and possibly other localities as far as the northeastern coast of Asia, including Japan. Now it is making a recovery and is found in small numbers from California to Alaska. It prefers rocky shallows and kelp beds and is seldom found more than a mile from shore.

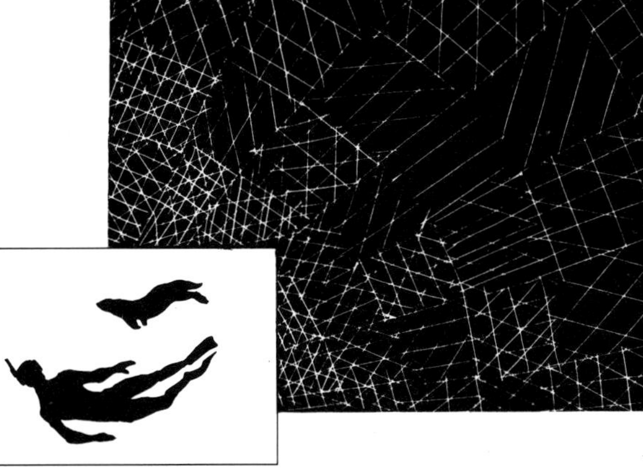

# SEA OTTERS

*(Enhydra lutra)*

Sea otters do not swim by instinct—they have to be taught. As illustrated in "The Lesson", the mothers lure their infants under the water with sea urchins. The young ones, or kits, nurse and play on their mothers' belly while she floats on her back. If alarmed she tucks her kit under her arm and submerges. When they sleep they wrap themselves tightly with a strand of kelp as a tether. The otters spend most of their lives in the water, going ashore only during the most severe storms. They are the only truly amphibious members of the weasel family.

Fun is an essential part of the otters' nature. They are even known to play with other sea animals such as seals and sea lions. This behavior contributes to their adaptation to life in the water. Play reinforces social behavior and helps perfect hunting and fighting skills. Another curious behavior is how they "stand" in the water and shade their eyes with their paws while looking for predators.

Sea otters dive for most of their food. They seek sea urchins, clams, mussels, and their favorite, abalone. After using stones to pry them loose from the ocean bottom, they cleverly bring up rocks to smash the mollusk shells on their chest. They eat while floating on their backs among the kelp. Other than the primates, otters are the only reported mammal to use a tool for foraging.

Tiny bubbles of air trapped in their fur serve as their only insulation and assist in flotation. The density of the fur reaches fifty thousand strands per square inch, the highest in the animal kingdom. They spend many hours preening to force the air into the fluffed up coat. If its texture is slicked down by oil from a spill, their fur will literally become waterlogged. If not remedied, this will cause the otters to die from exposure to cold.

At the turn of the century the entire species had been hunted to the brink of extinction until an international treaty in 1911 banned their exploitation. Abalone fishermen complained that the sea otters were depleting the abalone population, but ecologists maintain that they do not take enough to threaten the industry. Most likely any reduction in the fishermen's catch was due to overfishing and hunting. An interesting result of their past absence was an overabundance of sea urchins which began to choke off the oxygen and thereby threaten other forms of sea life—including abalone. The paradox was that the otter, by controlling the sea urchins, actually benefited the abalone industry which was bent on its elimination.

The sea otters were thought to be extinct in California until a small herd was discovered near Carmel at Big Sur in 1938. That population has made a slow comeback and now may number one thousand. The same is happening in other areas. Though they have made a marvelous comeback they may not exist in sufficient numbers to assure their ultimate survival.

# ORCAS BY NIGHT

In unison
Through the ink black night
Marauders
Of the hidden currents
And the dark depths,
Score the smoothness
Of the salty velvet
With their silent wake.

Warmblooded submarines
Cruise
In their royal band
Of conquering heroes,
Fearing no trespassers.

In royal procession,
Like kings and queens
They survey their domain.
Undisputed lords
In the Kingdom
Of the Seven Seas.

*Bruce C. Eriksen*

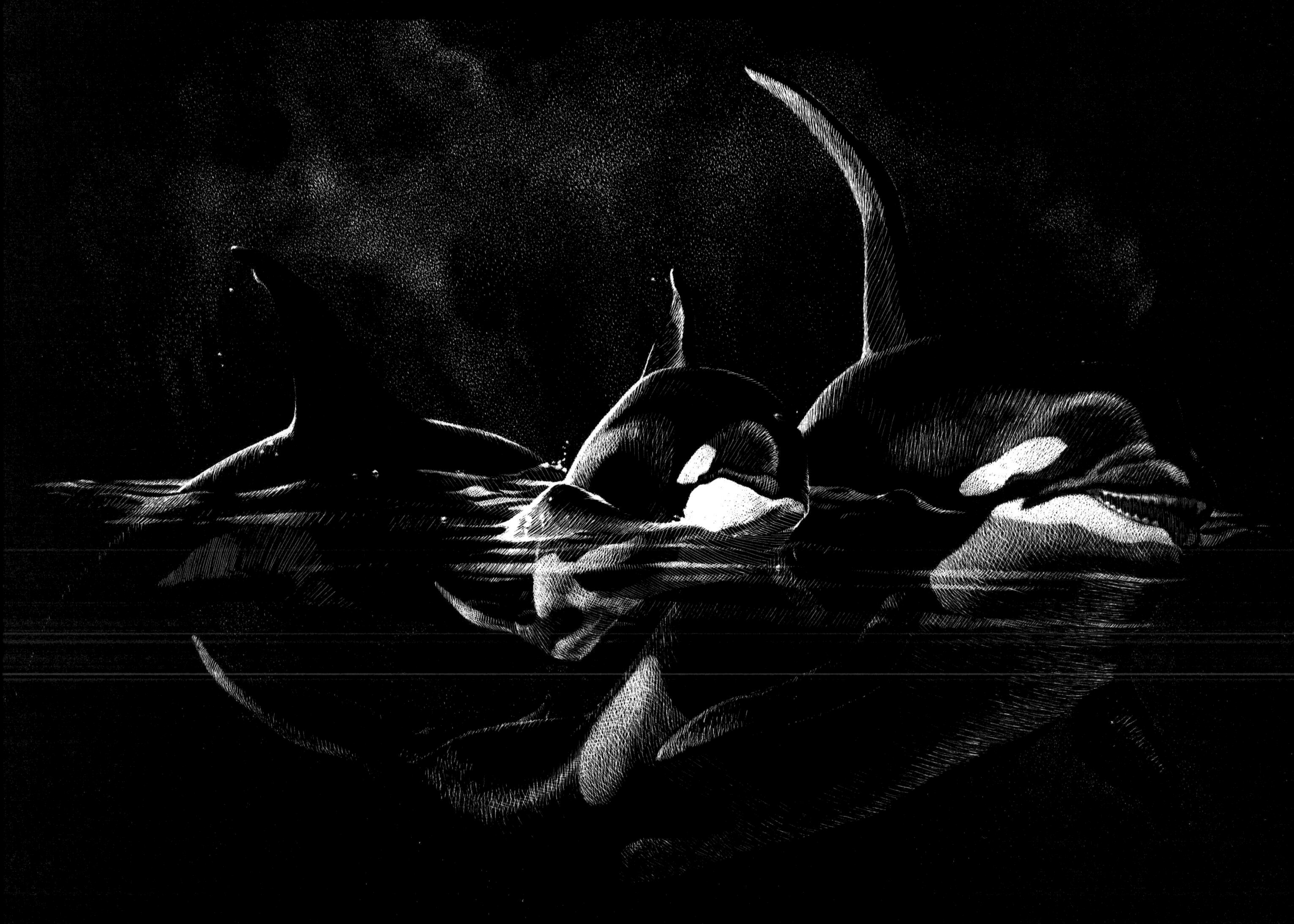

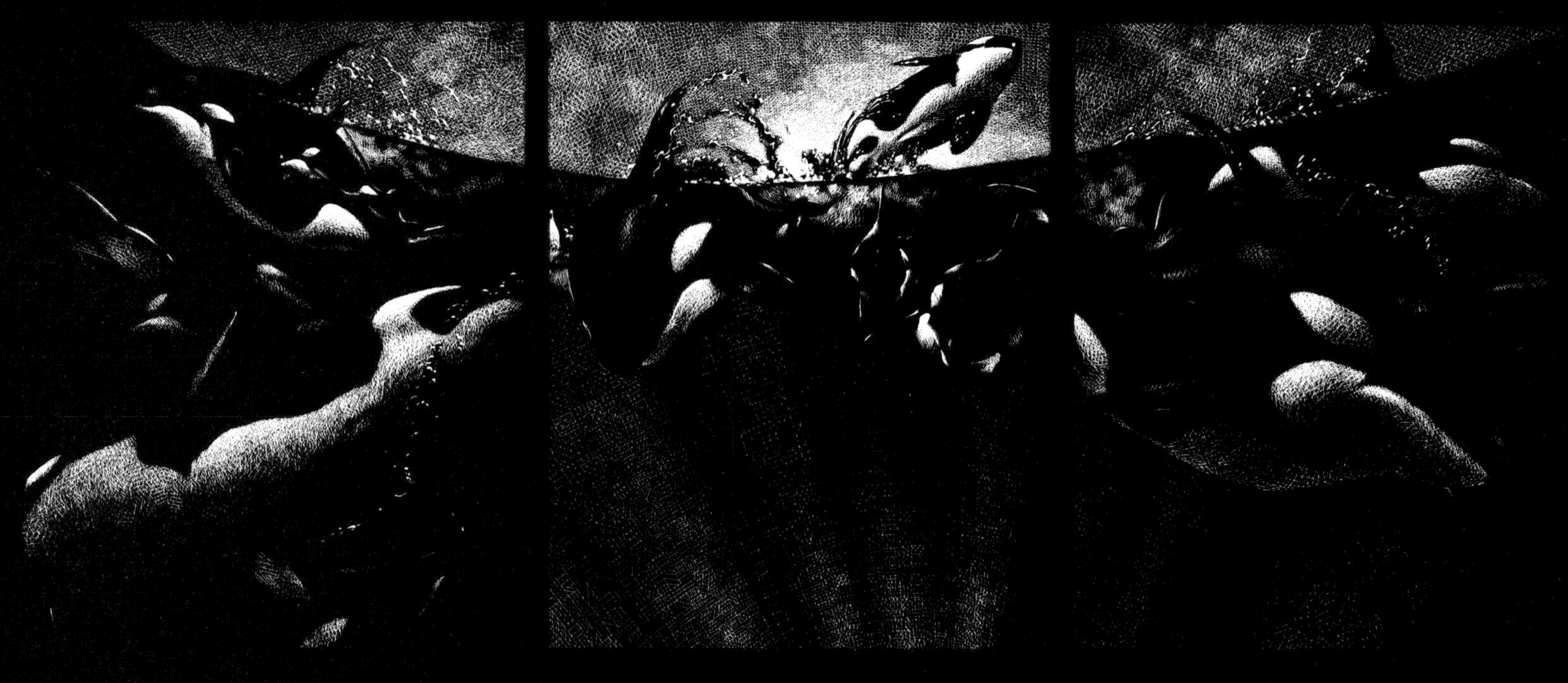

# SHIMMERING WATERS

The cavalcade
Of sleek dark torsos,
In turbulent exuberance,
Churning the sea
Into a tempest
Of foam and spray
Surrounded
And carried me
In the tow
Of their living tide.

I felt small,
Like a minnow
Tossed in the briny surf,
Until,
As quickly as they had come,
I was left awash
In the wake
Of their passing,
Once more alone
On the shimmering waters.

*Bruce C. Eriksen*

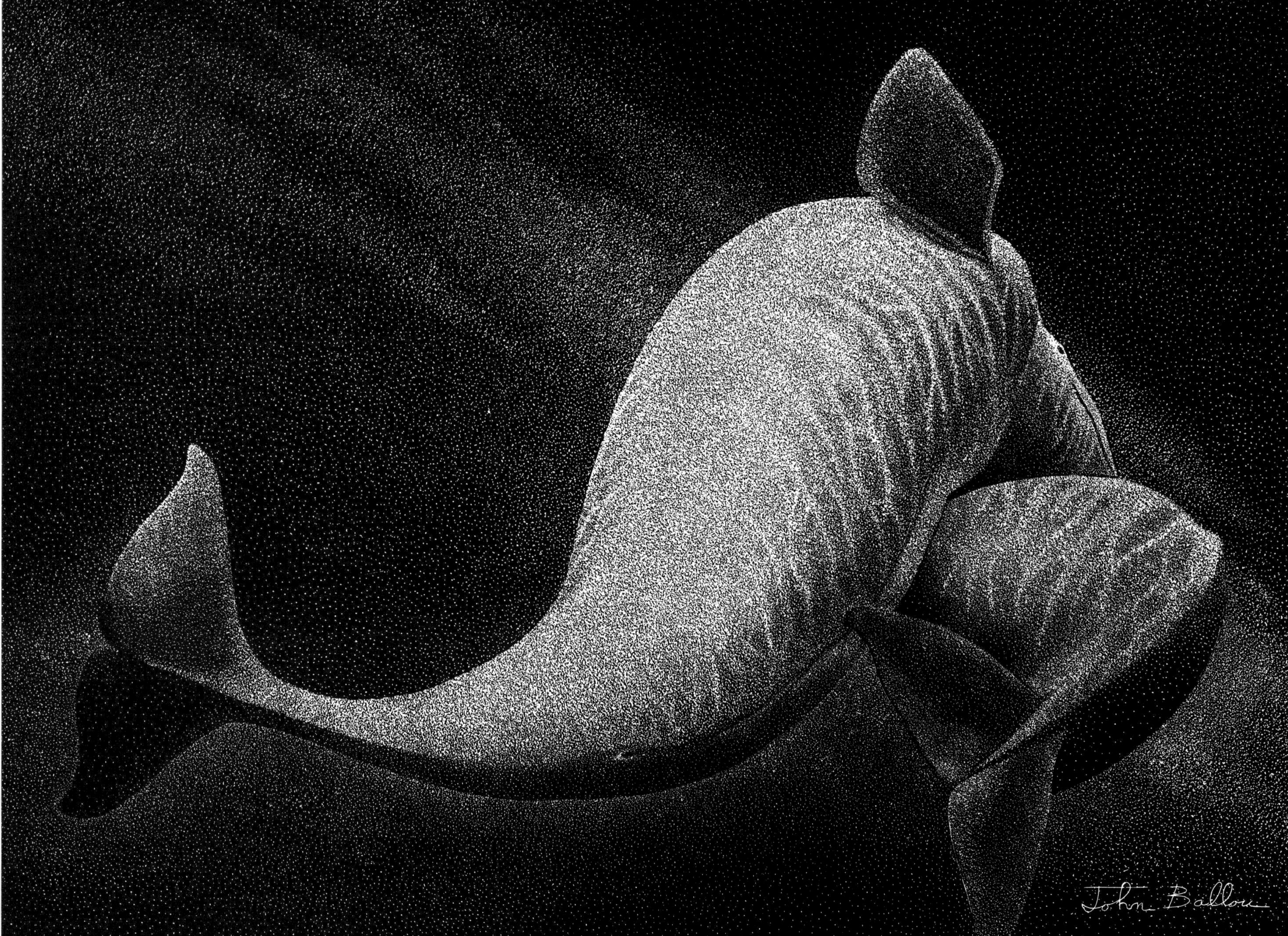
John Ballou

# EMBRACE

With a gentle caress
Our feelings encircle us
In a cocoon
Of our creation

Because,
We are partners
In the unfolding
Of our lives.

Our shared fortune
Binds us tightly
In a destiny
We are eager to accept.

For a moment
We drop our defenses
And mingle
In one another's atmosphere

And receive a warmth
Which could not exist
Without the bond
Of our love.

*Bruce C. Eriksen*

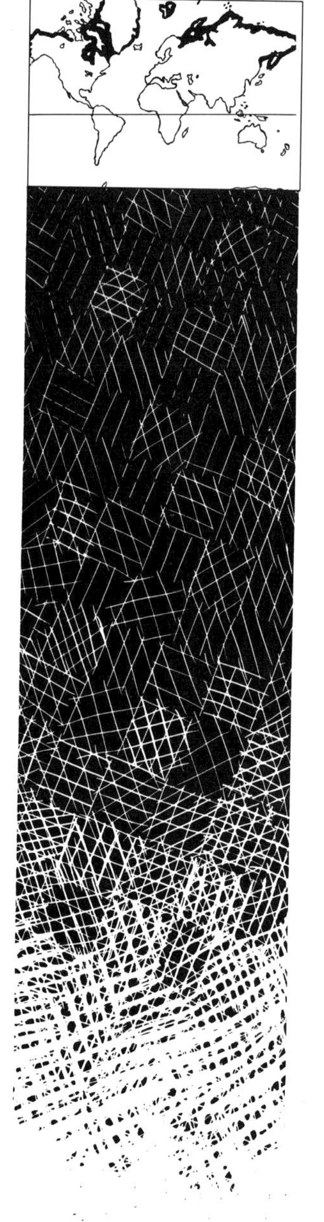

## *The Geographical Distribution of the Beluga*

The beluga's movement is confined to the arctic and subarctic waters of the Northern U.S.S.R., North America, and Greenland. Some populations are strongly migratory while others reside continuously in a well-defined area. Usually found near shore, the beluga is called a coastal species, though some are occasionally found in deep water. They are regularly observed in the St. Lawrence and Sequenay rivers in late spring and summer. Sightings have occurred as far as 1,100 kilometers up the Yukon River and the Saint Lawrence River to Quebec.

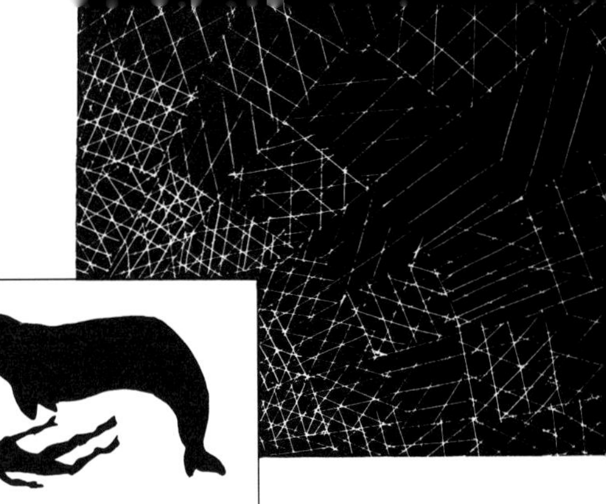

# BELUGA
*(Delphinapterus leucas)*

The beluga has been dubbed by sailors as the "Sea Canary" because its sound could be heard through the hulls of old sailing vessels. Its chirps, squeals, whistles, and clangs are very loud and may be heard in the air as well. The gregarious beluga, also called the white whale, has been observed in gatherings of more than one thousand, particularly in estuaries during the summer.

Its proportionally small head is supported by free cervical vertebrae. This arrangement allows it to nod and turn its head as few other whales may. Extra vertebrae in the belugas' spine allows them to contort their bodies around ice flows and to embrace, as in the illustration. The beluga is also capable of a wide variety of facial expressions. It smiles and purses its mouth with a flexibility that seems to serve it both for bottom feeding and for communication among its peers. A rounded "melon" which expressively changes shape overhangs the beak and adds to its uniquely characteristic look. In the wild it is not as naturally demonstrative in swimming behavior as are some other whales, and it does not usually leap except when trained to do so in captivity.

Predictable migratory behavior has made the belugas vulnerable to hunting. The whales have been severely depleted historically by over-exploitation. Local fishermen have used the technique of driving them ashore in groups. Trawl nets have been used extensively for harvest by the Soviet Union and Japan. Native whalers in Alaska, Greenland, and Canada hunt them with harpoons and rifles. Oil, mukluk, and meat are the principle commercial by-products and *porpoise leather* was manufactured from white whale skins during the early twentieth century.

Commercial hunting has been ended by every country except the Soviet Union, and native hunting still continues to put pressure on the beluga's remaining numbers. The beluga's affinity for the shallow coastal areas further complicates its survival. Habitat alteration (due to artificial island building, pipeline construction, oil tanker and ice breaker traffic, and hydroelectric dams which change water temperature and flow in the polar regions) is now a major threat and is becoming possibly more of a problem than hunting. This confuses the beluga's migration and mating patterns.

Especially dramatic is the plight of the belugas who live in the Saint Lawrence River Basin who share the environment with industry and its toxic waste. A government-funded autopsy program turned up very high levels of 24 different contaminants in the white whales' flesh. Levels of PCBs were so high that, under Canadian law, their corpses should be treated as hazardous waste. Other toxins found were DDT, heavy metals, Mirex (a pesticide), hexachlorobenzene, and polyaromatic hydrocarbons. These pollutants caused cases of extensive pulmonary fibrosis, transitional cell carcinoma, granulosa cell tumor, haemangioma of the bladder, and perforated ulcers. The list goes on. The population in that area has dropped from an estimated 5,000 individuals in the 1800's to about 500, perhaps less than 350, in present times. The effect that this degree of pollution is having on other sea life, land animals, and humans in the same area is no doubt very serious. Presently it is questionable how much is being accomplished to remedy the situation. The poisoning goes on.

# THE TRACKER

You steal
Across the uncomfortable
Starkness
Of the open.

You know
That it is safe
Among the bushes,
Where you are
An undiscernible blur
On nature's canvas.

But you must go.
Your senses have been sparked
By the call of your prey.

You ache to move,
But you wait ...
Interminably.
Failure has taught you
Patience.

Finally ...
When the instant arrives,
Your tense muscles uncoil
In a clawing, clutching pounce
And that life
Becomes yours.

The hunt ...
The capture ...
Resolution.
You have fulfilled
Your destiny.

*Bruce C. Eriksen*

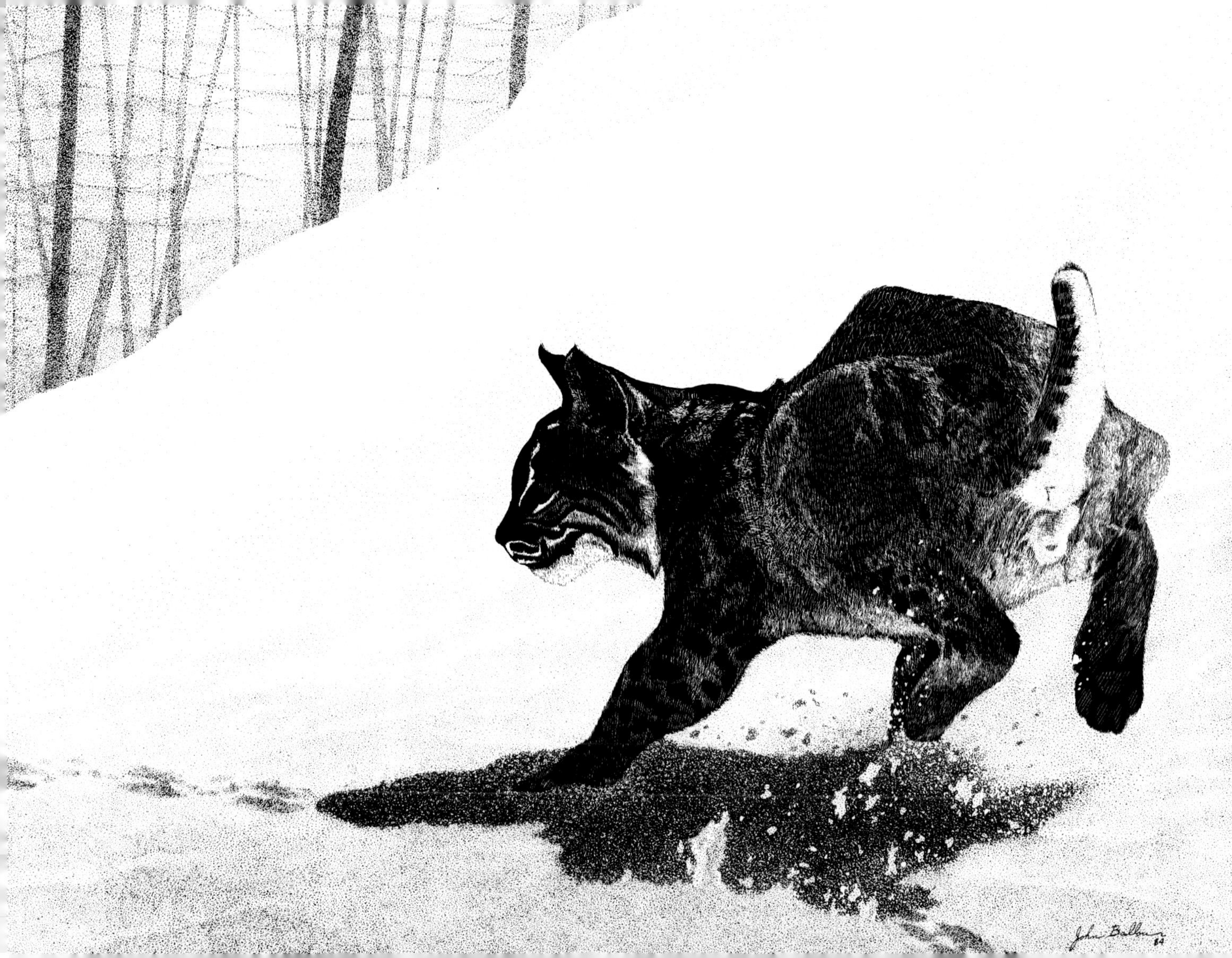

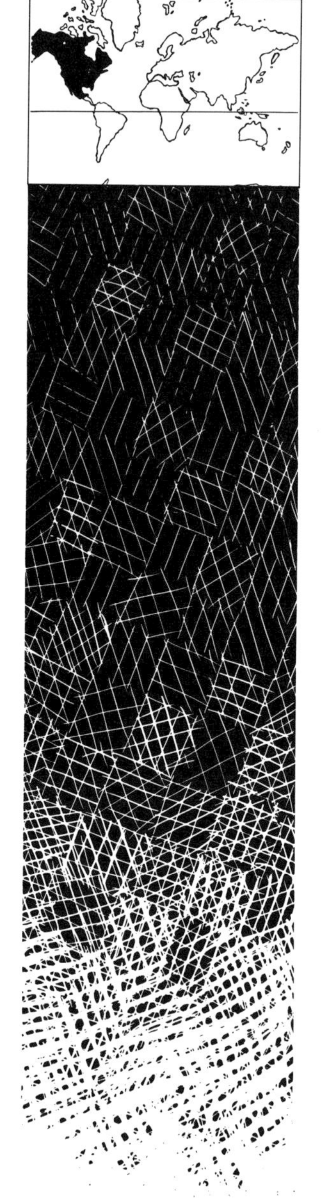

# *The Geographical Distribution of the Bobcat*

The most common wildcat in North America, the bobcat lives in scattered populations throughout most of the United States and southern Canada. It is most abundant in the far west and most absent in the central and lower midwest, especially in densely populated agricultural regions such as the San Joaquin Valley in California.

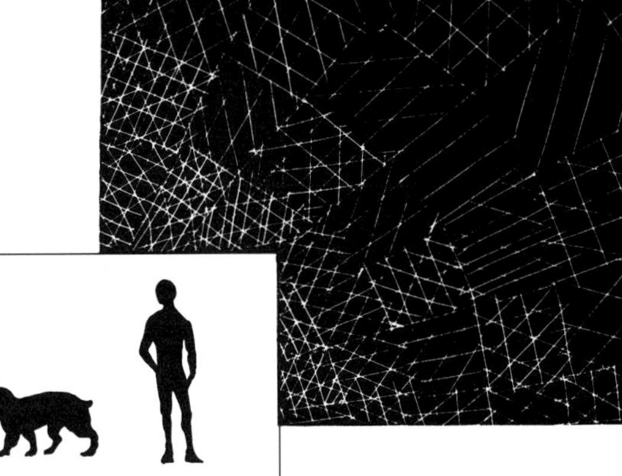

# BOBCAT

*(Lynx rufus)*

The bobcat is a daytime hunter. Its black-spotted brown coat blends well with the background of thickets and rocks where it waits to pounce on small game like rabbits, hares, small rodents, cave bats, and porcupines. Lynx rufus is often found in trees where it seeks security and advantage. As a habit the cat repeatedly traces the same pathway, making it easier to find its most successful hunting grounds. However, this habit also makes it easier for its own predator, man, to find it.

This small cat is still killed for its fur which is used for clothing trim. The bobcat is also a favorite subject for taxidermists because of it fearsomely handsome looks. Due to its wiliness it is not endangered in less populated areas. There its population is stable and increasing, but, in those areas highly populated and extensively cultivated, bobcats are persecuted and pushed out. In 1977 85,000 bobcats were harvested for their skins by commercial trappers. One reason for this onslaught is that the bobcat sometimes preys on domestic animals.

The bobcat is an excellent example of a small, highly adaptable species. Year round breeding habits and relish for abundant animals such as the jack rabbit facilitate its own survival and serve to control potentially destructive pests. The species can successfully compete despite natural and minor infringements on its territory, but eventually the species cannot compete with the population density of expanding urban centers and increased land cultivation. Consequently it is pressed further back into more restricted areas. These already taxed habitats will only support a limited number of species. Therefore, encroachment by man means the thinning of population and the starvation of other species which compete for the same game. In the areas where the bobcat used to control potential pests, the balance is upset, and threats to agriculture such as rabbits and rodents are left unchecked. Farmers and urbanites are then forced to resort to dangerous methods of control such as toxic pesticides, which have their own consequences.

With the weakening of every individual link in a chain carefully planned by nature, the chain's ultimate strength is imperiled. A complete break is always more costly than the less expensive sacrifice that could have prevented it. As man "tames" the world and marvels at his own accomplishments, little by little he is also becoming aware of the blunders of his impatience. If man learns from his history he will realize that quick cures have only led to temporary patches holding back the awesome force of nature. Even a small carnivore like a cat and its humble prey the rabbit do their part to check the formidable, destructive power of the abundant rodents who control the insects. We do not stand alone in our struggle to survive: the bobcat is but one in a network of our allies.

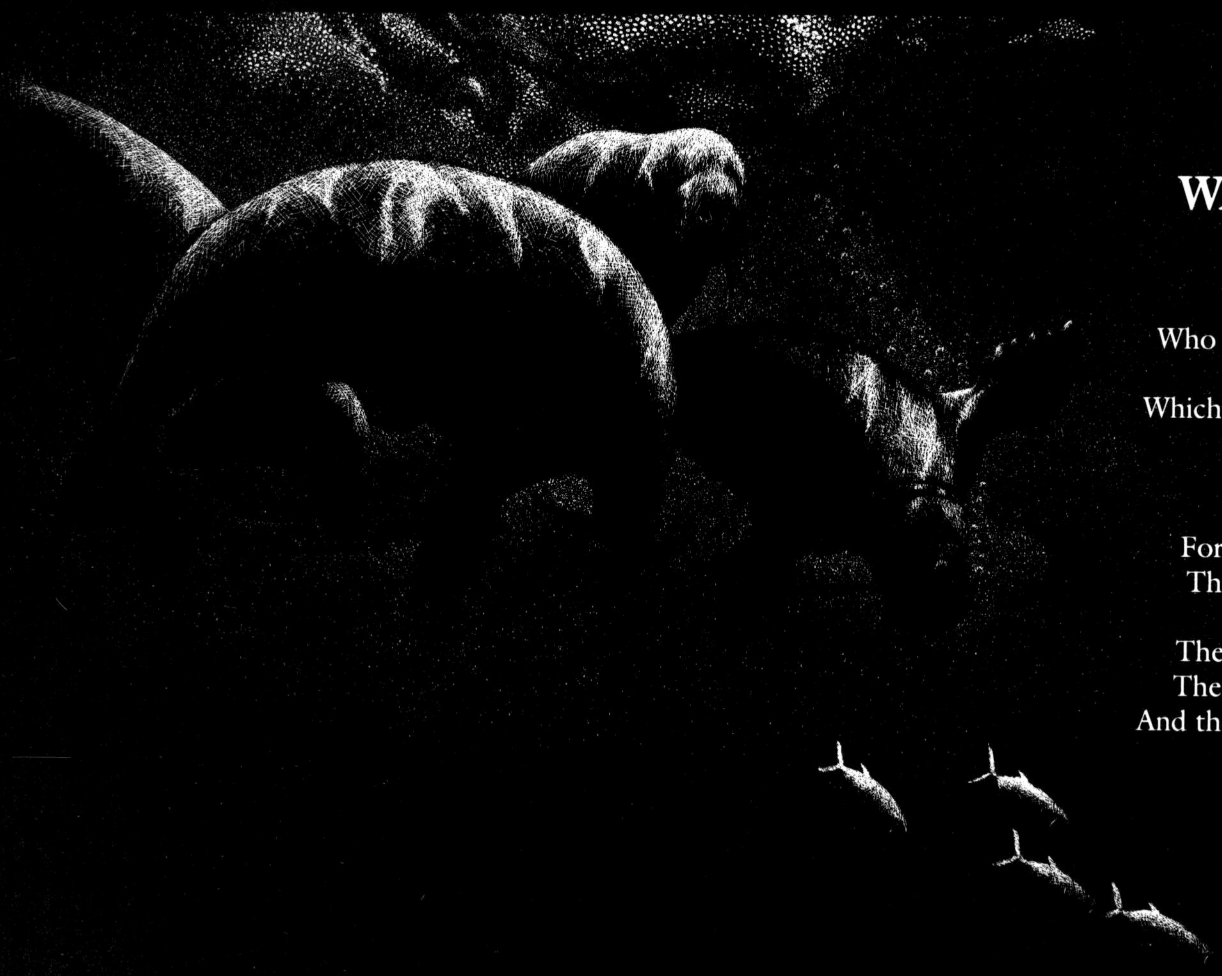

# WALRUS HUNT

To the Eskimos
Who understand and worship you,
Your mass,
Which lumbers across sparse icy rock
And slides
On frigid white terrain,
Is still desired
For those venerable properties
That make you so vulnerable.

The pure density of your tusks,
The fleshy reservoir of your oil,
And the durable texture of your hide,
Separate you and them
From the relentless
Brunt of nature.

To the greedy
You are a corpulent prize
Which undulates on the land—
A target for their pleasure.
They carve trophies out of you
Discarding the rest,
Their waste—
Your life.

While they may marvel
At your unconquerable expression
As you protect your kingdom,
Which lies on the edge
Between above and down under,
They scar
And divide your continent
With their progress.

Can they not see
That your very existence
Is a monument
To the positive force
Which perpetuates
What to them
Seems a barren wasteland,
But to you
Is a teeming garden?

*Bruce C. Eriksen*

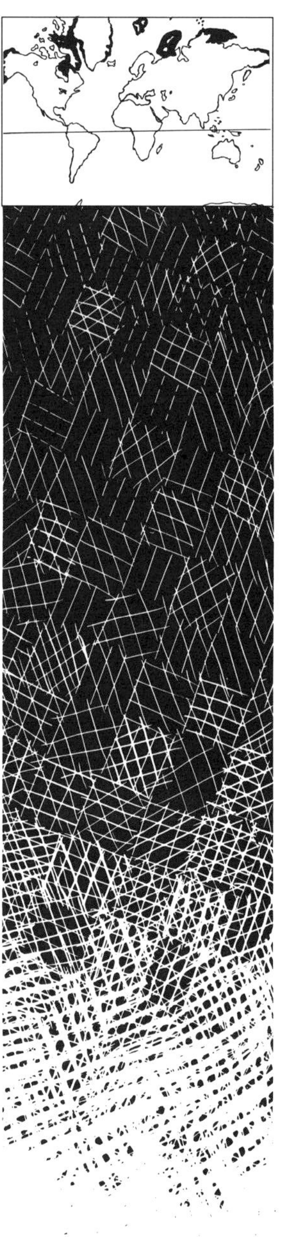

# *The Geographical Distribution of The Walrus*

The walrus lives in the arctic seas, from East Canada and Greenland to North Eurasia and West Alaska. It has two distinct populations or races, the Atlantic and the Pacific. The Atlantic race is found from Greenland southward and westward to the Hudson Bay. The Pacific race is found in the Chukchi Sea in the summer and in the Bering Sea off Southwest Alaska in the winter.

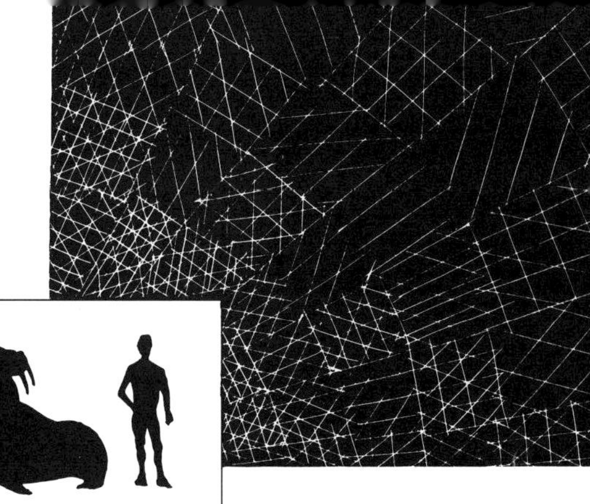

# WALRUS

*(Odobenus rosmarus)*

The walrus is the most important animal in the life of the Eskimo, in much the same way that the buffalo was to the American Indians. Eskimos use them in ingenious ways for survival. The hides are used for kayak boat covers and clothing, the blubber for oil and fuel, and the tusks for sled runners and tools. Now, with the introduction of modern weapons and technology, one of the only remaining "uses" of the tusks is scrimshaw, decorated ivory, which is still a source of revenue. Kayaks are almost a thing of the past because the native population has access to modern boats.

The walrus is one of the largest sea-going mammals. The males grow to as long as twelve feet and weigh on the average sixteen hundred pounds. The Pacific variety is the largest. Because they are hairless they depend on their tremendous bulk of blubber to keep them warm.

Though clumsy on land, walrus are fluid swimmers easily able to swim fifteen miles per hour. They can dive as deep as three hundred feet and stay submerged for as long as thirty minutes. Because of the murky nature of the ocean floor, the touch of their hairy muzzle is used to locate food. The ability to squirt water out of their mouth at high pressures is well known to zoo keepers. In the wild, squirting assists in excavation for food in the silt on the ocean bottom. They can easily eat one hundred pounds of food in a day or, if necessary, survive for a week without feeding.

The impressive appearance of the male is all the more remarkable because of his tusks which grow up to forty inches long. Female tusks are shorter and more curved. Occasionally the tusks are used to stab seals. A formidable weapon, the size of the tusk helps to establish dominance during mating. Usually they are used for digging up food from the ocean bottom and scraping seafood from the rocks.

The walrus is extremely sociable, often gathering in herds of two thousand or more. When conditions are crowded on land they are quite happy to haul out onto other walruses. The bulls, young males, and females separate only during the mating season when the bulls herd their females and defend them vigorously. The herd spends much time sunning and sleeping on rocks but they can also rest and sleep at sea supported vertically by air sacks in their necks.

The Marine Mammal Protection Act of 1972 forbids the hunting of the walrus except for the personal use of the Eskimo. However, the high value of the ivory and commercial demand for scrimshaw unfortunately creates a strong black market for the tusks, which means death for many of the population. The author and artists highly recommend heavy reconsideration when possibly buying artifacts made from the bodies of any wild species. The knowledge that those ornaments are leading to that species elimination should be motivation enough to abstain. We soon may have no more elephants in the wild because they possess high quality ivory. May we not let the same happen to the walrus.

# AFRICAN PELICANS

White winged cloud
Descending,
A mirror of wet lands
Stretches on.
Feather and foot
Touch down as one,
A vast lake of plenty,
All that we need
And more,
Shore to shore.
Clouds engage
The sun and wind.
This must go on forever.
Yet the sun besieges every day,
Soon enough
To have its way.
I feel restless somehow.
I feel I must move on,
White winged cloud
Ascending,
Then gone.

*John Ballou*

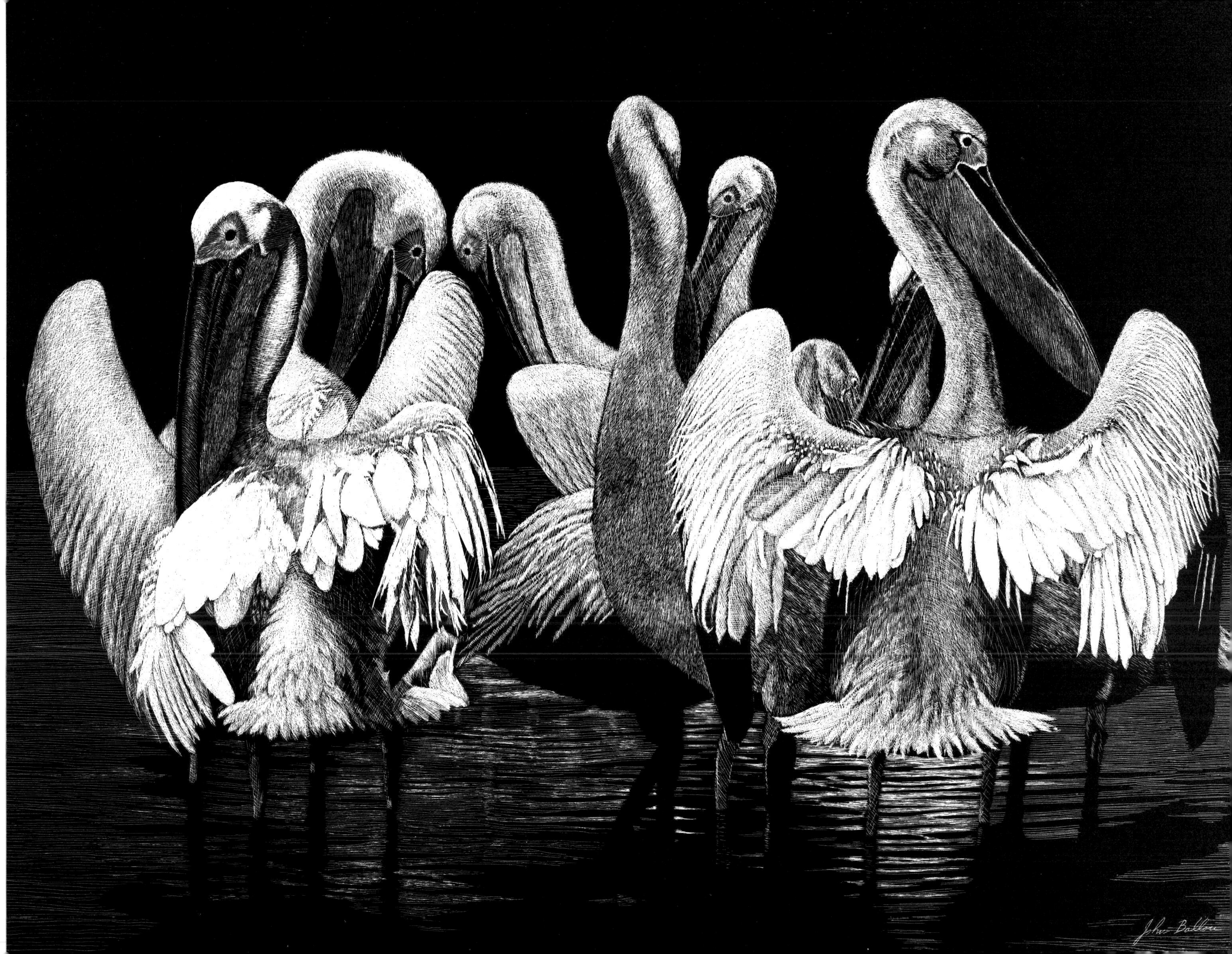
John Ballou

# HUMPBACK AND CALF

Listen to our song
My little one
As I sing
Its tidings to you.

It tells of the force
Of our life
And how we expand in waves
To all directions.

Begun by the most ancient,
The greatest of your ancestors,
Our message has slowly evolved
On its passage through time.

It has echoed
On familiar reefs
And mingled
In the faceted nuances
Of those who have gone before.

It has careened
Down unexplored canyons,
Pierced the fathoms
And has been taught
By the changing tide.

Remember our song,
My little one,
And weave
Its meaning well,

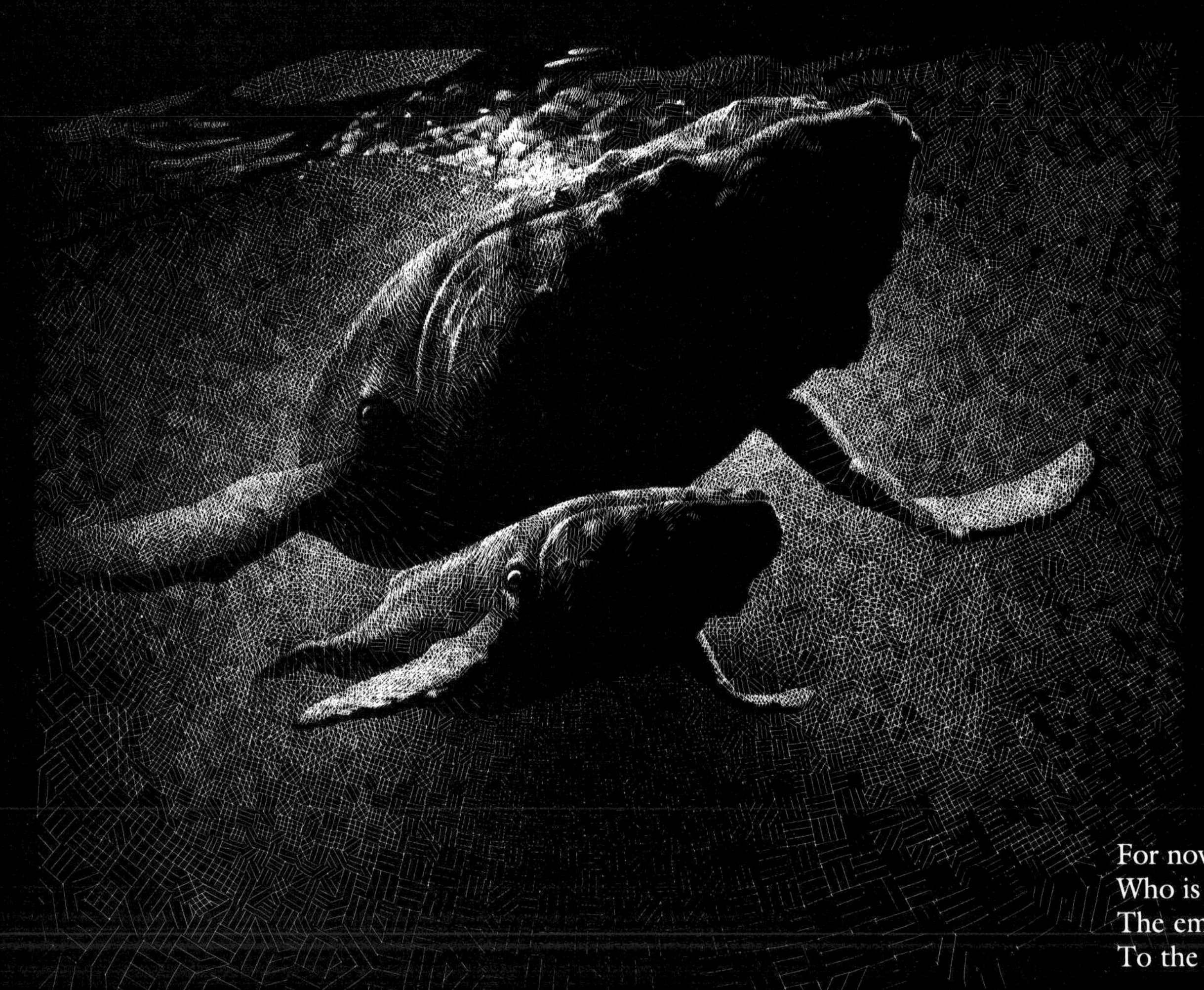

For now it is you
Who is the link,
The emissary,
To the next generation.

Sing,
Let me know
That when I am only
A crease in time
Your children
Will carry on.

*Bruce C. Eriksen*

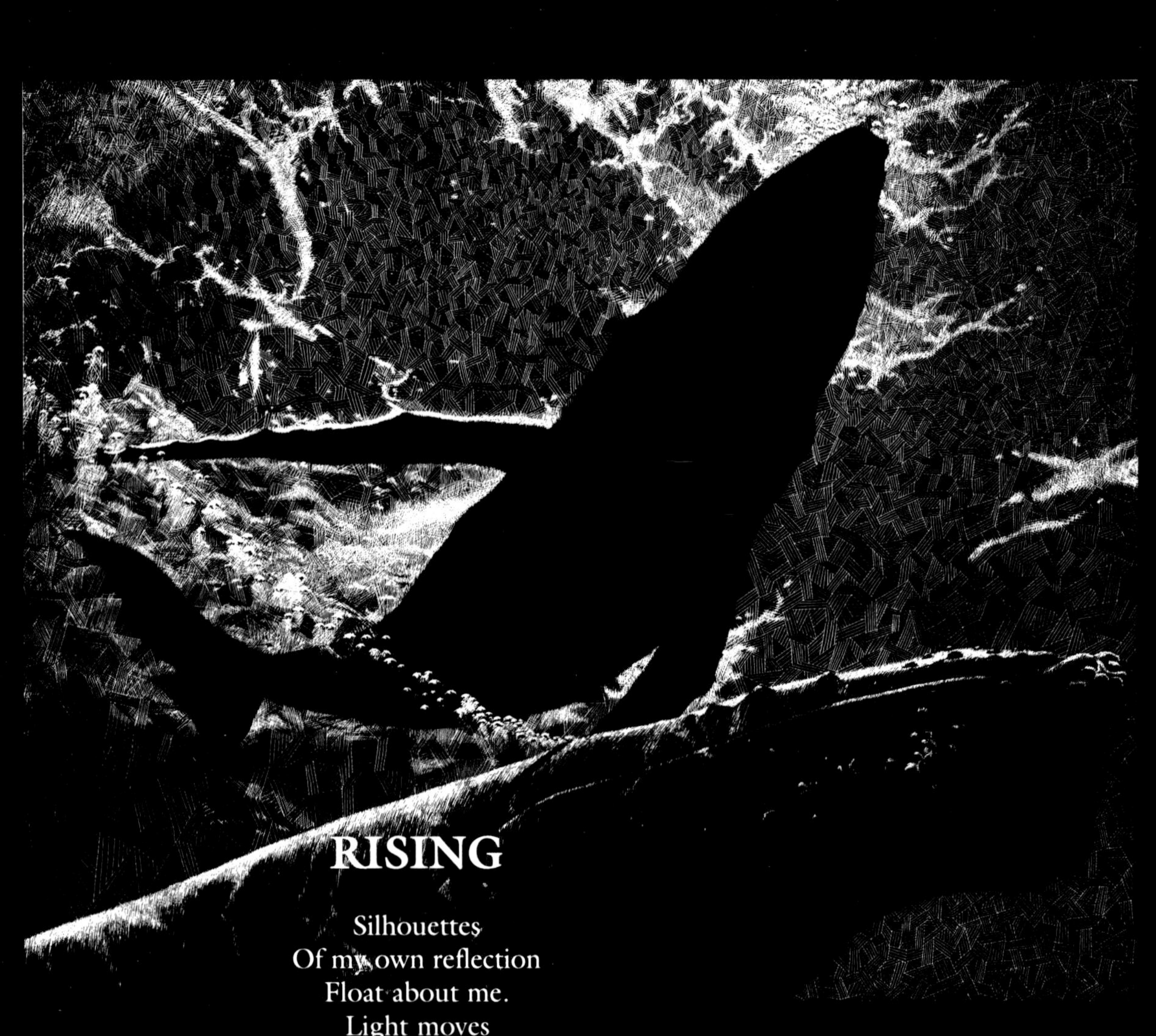

# RISING

Silhouettes
Of my own reflection
Float about me.
Light moves

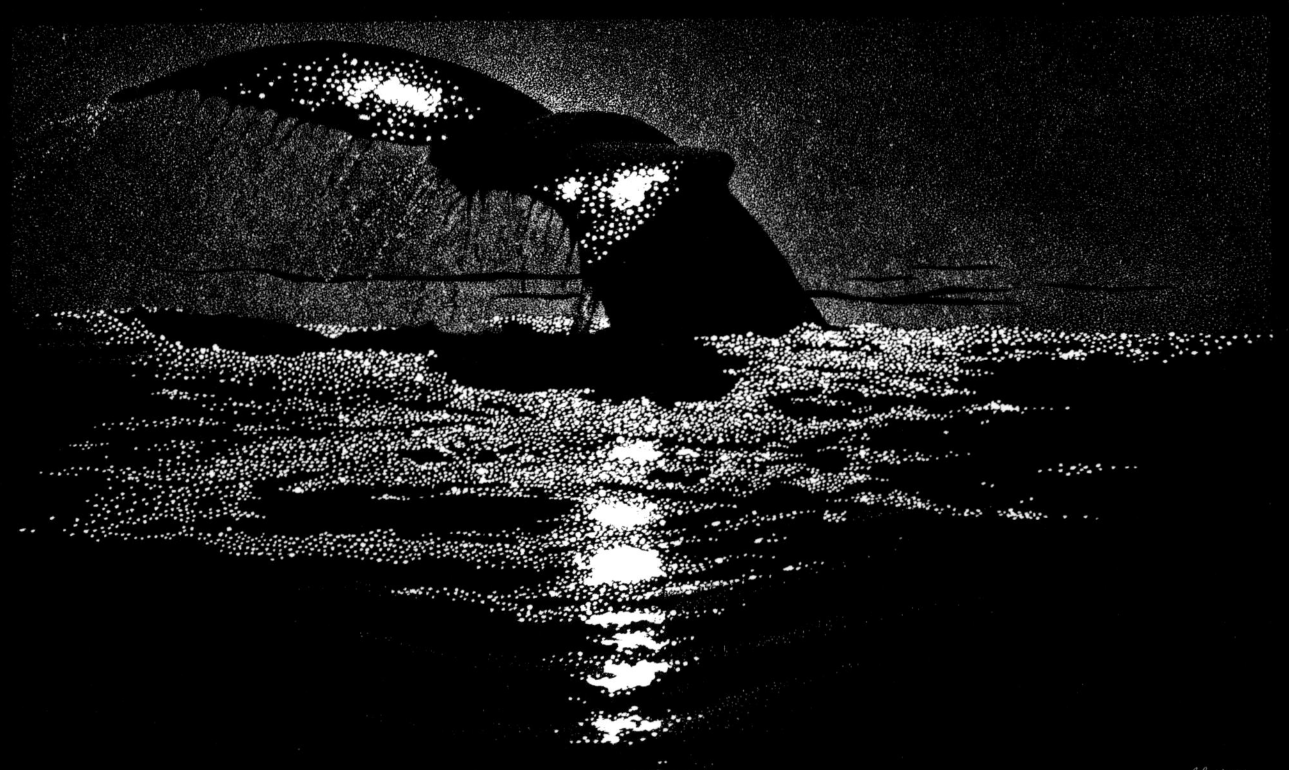
John Ballou

# METAMORPHOSIS

The ritual begins
As the Sun and Moon
Exert their moods
Of dark and light.

The current touches
The land and sea
With the force
Of its potent influence.

Transported
By the spell
Of our imagination,
On a wave
Of mystic evolution,

Equus,
Who grazes emerald pastures,
And the narwhal,
Who combs indigo ranges,

Merge in a vision
Of lucid truth
And unbounding freedom...
The Unicorn.

*Bruce C. Eriksen*

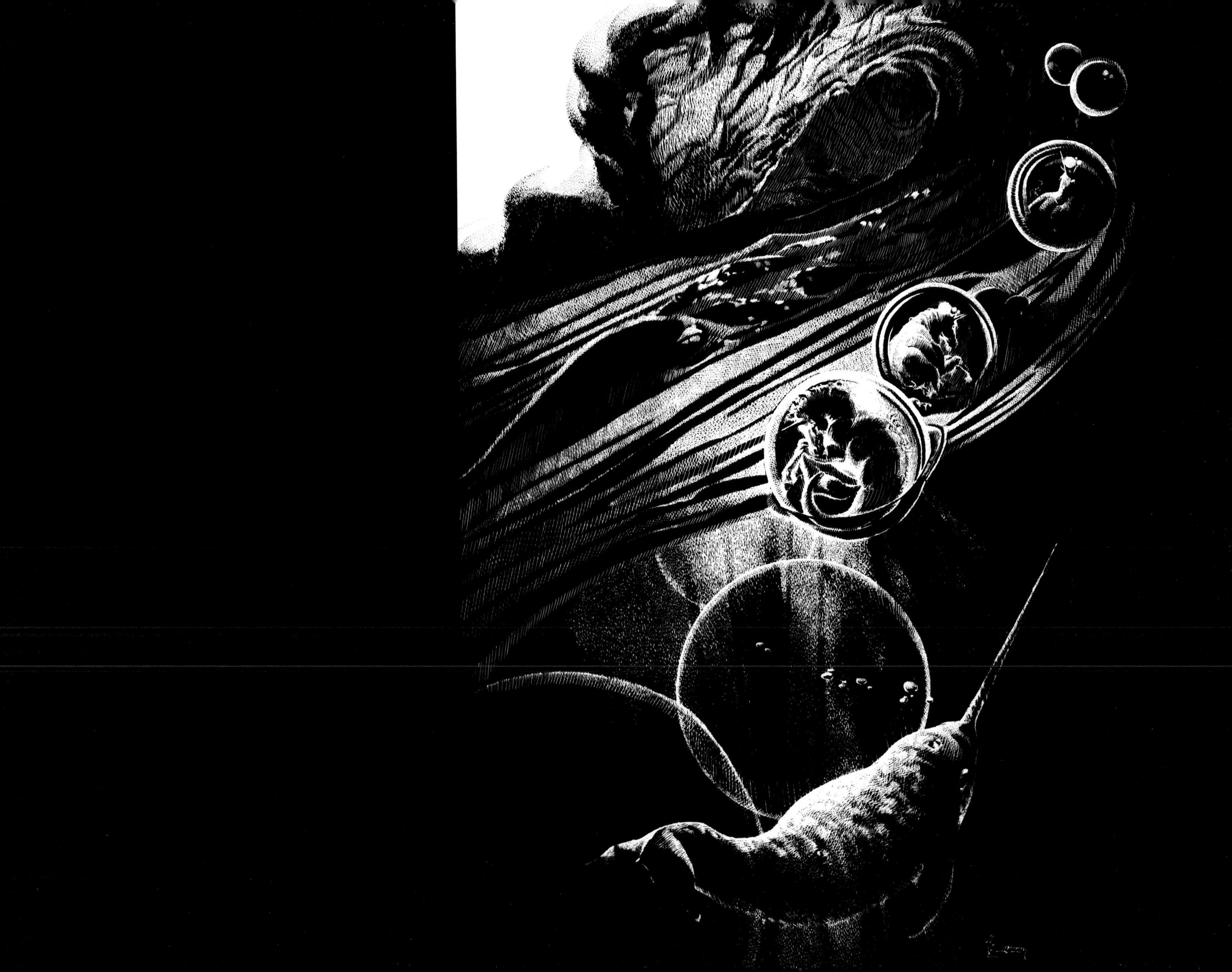

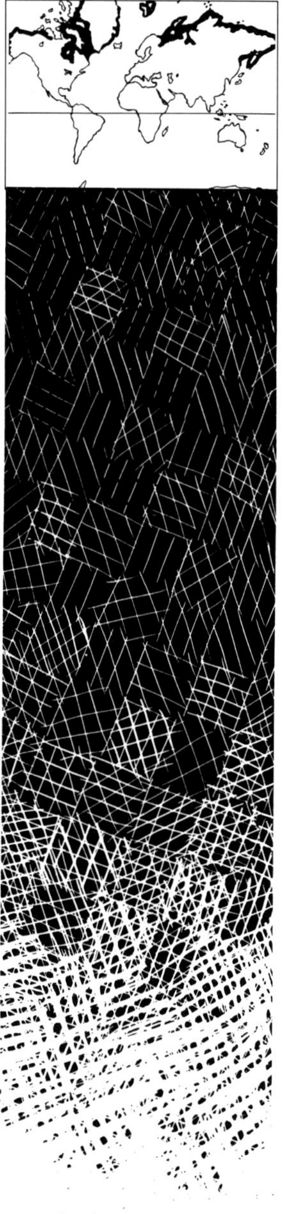

# *The Geographical Distribution of the Narwhal*

Narwhals are not often found far from the loose ice pack. Therefore their movement is predictable relative to seasonal ice formation and drift. Narwhals are abundant in the high Arctic, but there is no reliable count of their numbers. It is rare for them to be found outside of the Arctic Sea. Their range is generally around 70 degrees north, about the level of Norway and Point Barrow, Alaska. Narwhals occasionally stray farther south and have been stranded on the coasts of Britain and Holland. Several thousand may exist in the Soviet Arctic. In the summer they penetrate deep into the polar ice pack to bear their young.

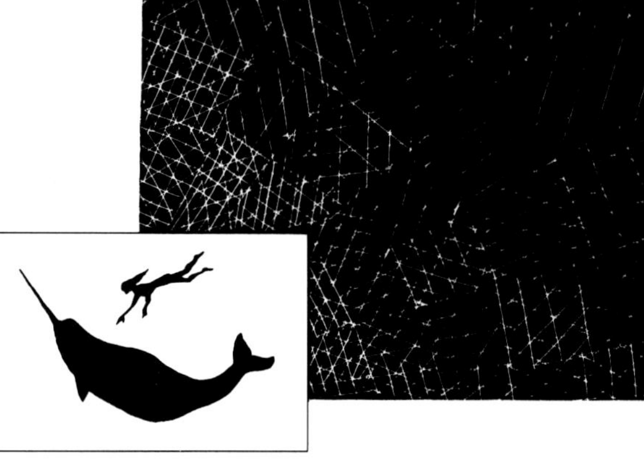

# ARCTIC NARWHAL

*(Monodon monoceros)*

The narwhal is famous for the long spiraling single tusk found on the males. This spectacular appendage, which often reaches ten feet, has earned the narwhal the name "Unicorn of the Sea" and has contributed to the whale's rarity. The narwhal used to be seen regularly in waters as far south as mid-Labrador, but it has since been depleted from those waters because of the greed for its horn. In addition to being beautiful, the tusk is believed by some of its human predators to have magic and medicinal powers. Now it is illegal even to have possession of a tusk in the United States and in some other countries, but the ivory unfortunately brings high profit to collectors and apothecaries in Asian countries.

The horn is actually one of the only two teeth the otherwise toothless narwhals have which protrude through the gum. It has been speculated that the three meter horn is used for hunting food by scraping ice flows or grubbing on the sea bottom. More recent observations of the narwhal's behavior leads scientists to believe that it may be used for sparring during the mating season. The narwhal sometimes "stands" in the water with head and horn exposed to the air, as if to display its prowess. Normally, however, the species is shy and rarely seen.

In the waters of west Greenland and the eastern Canadian Arctic, the local natives inflict heavy casualties on the reluctant creature. A resurgence in its popularity due to the ivory trade and to the unicorn myth may push the narwhal to the brink of extinction. Public outcry is increasingly putting pressure on worldwide markets for ivory. The large market of Taiwan has recently added laws of protection, but, until more markets for exotic vanishing species are cut off, poaching and exploitation will continue. The pursuit of the narwhal is an example of how man's greed for the possession of something so beautiful and rare has turned into a tragic worldly loss for all of us and for our children's children.

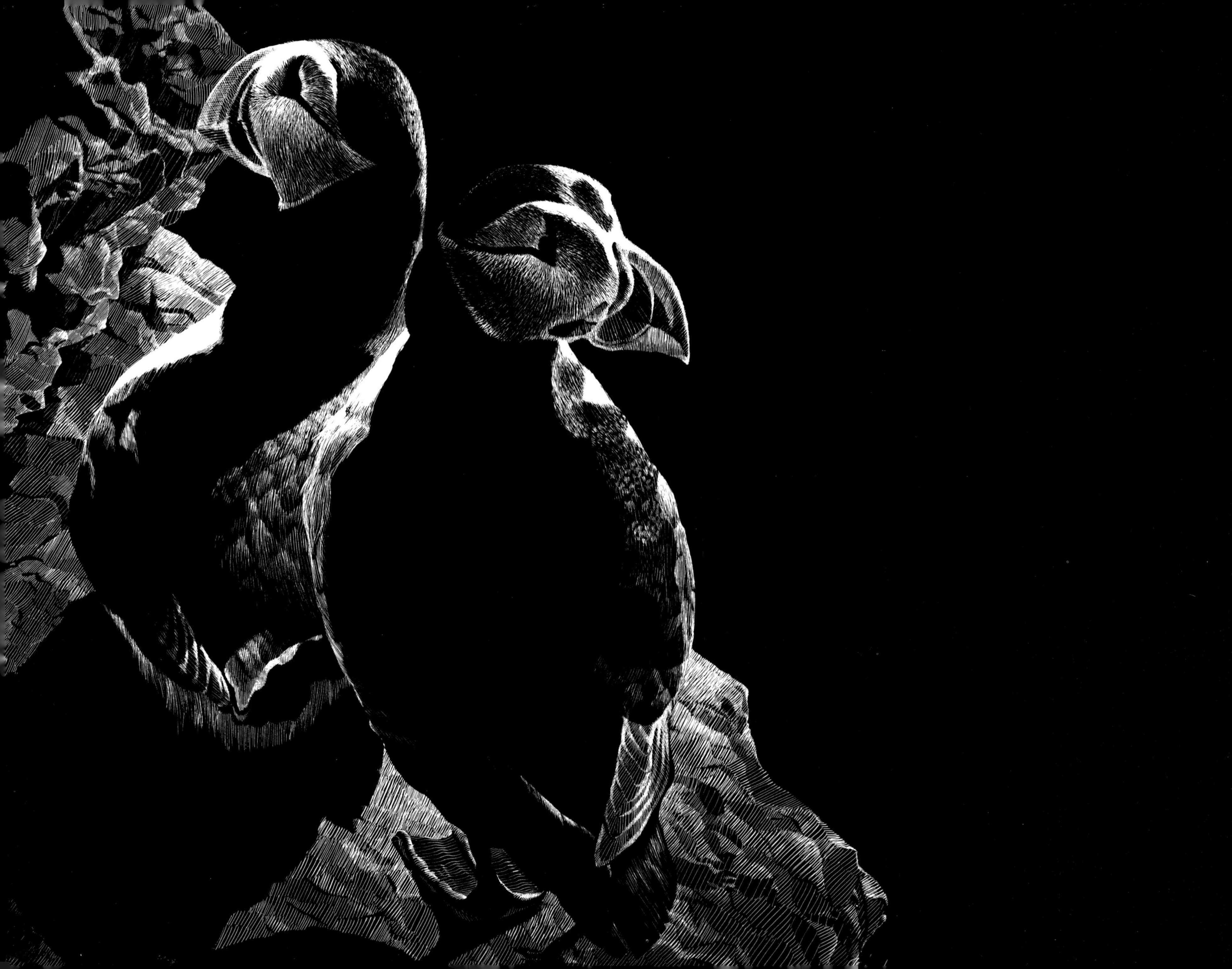

# TWO PUFFINS

On land
You waddle
To the edge
Of your precipice
And beat your wings
Faster, and faster,
Until by sheer persistence

You rise,
Still awkward,
But, making way,
They take you straightaway
To the water
Where wings become oars,
And feet, paddles.

Submerged,
You are an acrobat,
Who, in that gaudiest of beak,
Stacks innumerable fish
Neatly
In row after row

For the return home
To those craggy heights
Where you will continue
The ritual
Of your comic dance.

*Bruce C. Eriksen*

# TRUMPETER SWAN AND CYGNETS

A brassy choir
Blares forth from the sky
Trumpeting the eminent arrival
Of the great white fowl
Who stretch forth long necks
From the snowy fleece
Of their feather breasts
Between the powerful extended strokes
Of their grand wings.

The band of brash angels
Swoop down
Into the scurry
Of downy fledgling cygnets
Who awkwardly await the time
When they will rise
From their earthbound hatchery
And join in flawless
Symmetrical flight.

*Bruce C. Eriksen*

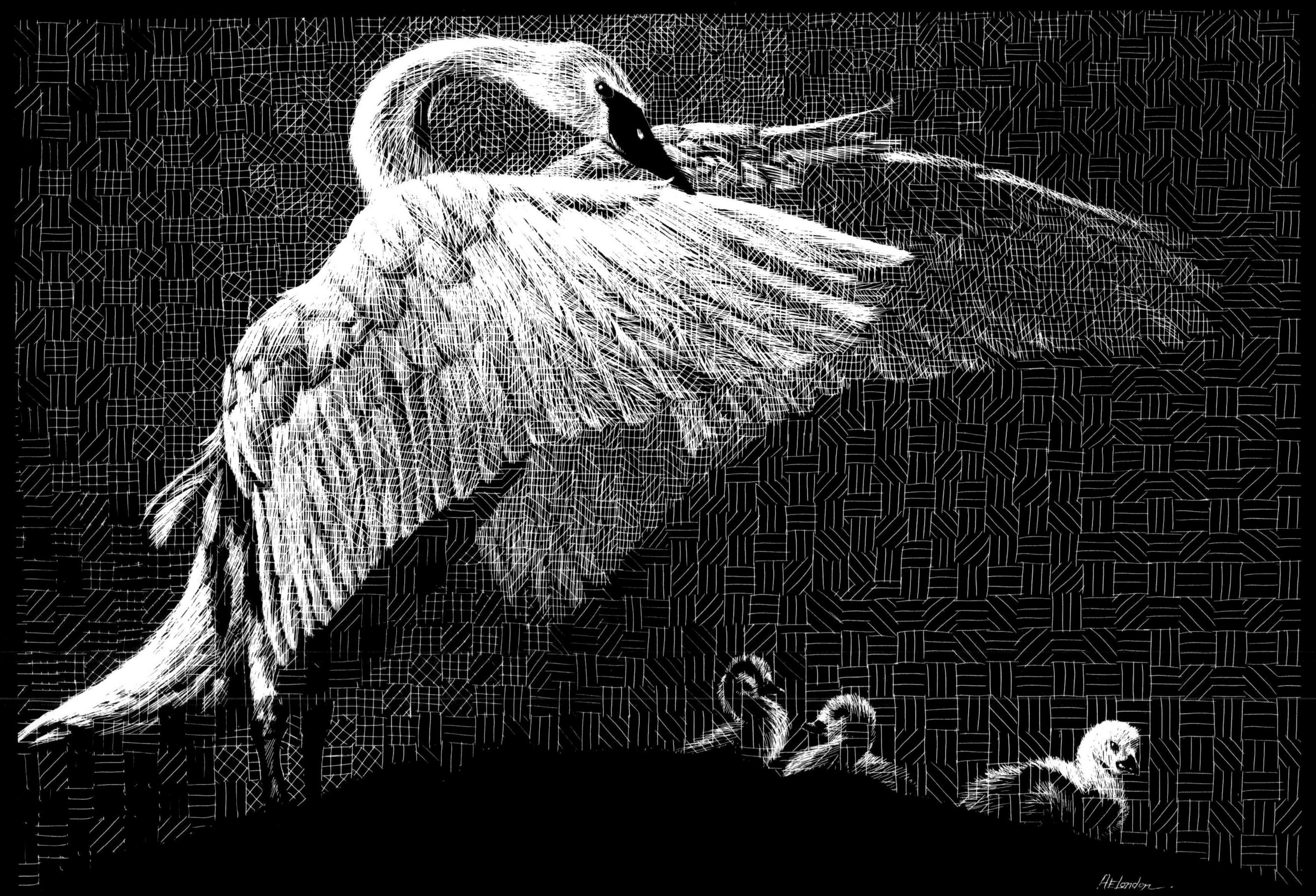
AE London

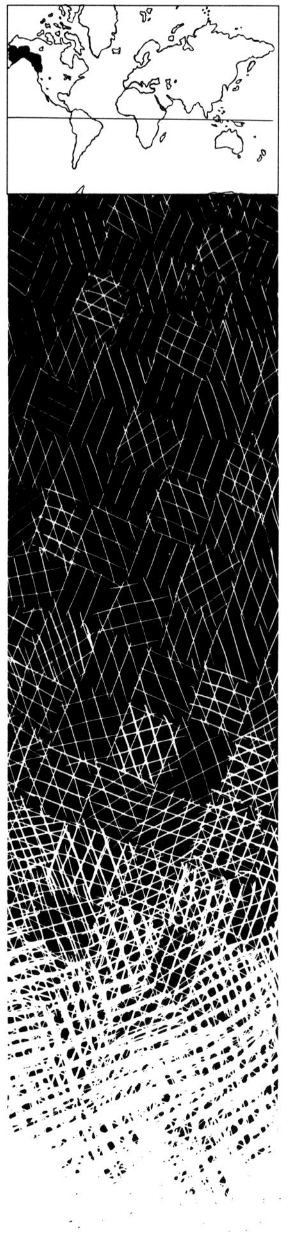

# *The Geographical Distribution of the Trumpeter Swan*

The trumpeter swan used to breed across the North American Continent as far south as Nova Scotia and as far east as Newfoundland. Now they are mostly concealed in the remote lake valleys of Alaska and British Columbia.

Others have been transfered to Wyoming, Oregon, Nevada, and South Dakota with success. The Hennepin Parks System in Minnesota has raised about 85 tame and wild swans over the past 20 years. Their goal is to have 100 free flying swans, with 15 nesting pairs in south central Minnesota, where they were once abundant in the 1800's.

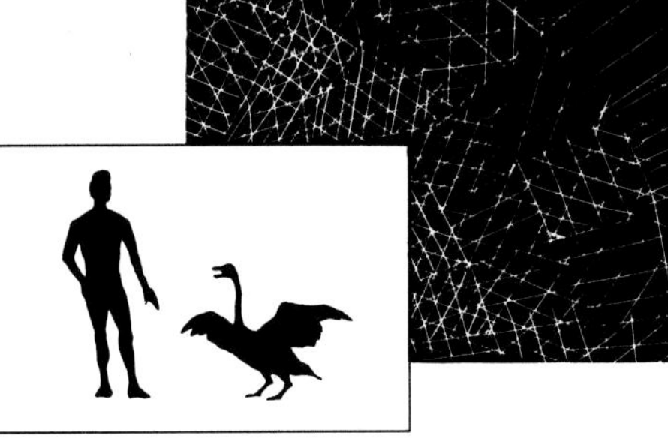

# TRUMPETER SWAN

*(Cygnus Buccinator)*

The trumpeter swan was named for its booming trumpet-like calls. The beauty of this bird's flight is an inspirational sight. The swan stretches out its elongated neck before its eight foot wingspan which beats in powerful extended strokes. Unfortunately many hunters get a great thrill out of shooting this magnificent creature.

The swan was slaughtered for its meat but more extensively for its densely feathered breasts. They were valued in the millinery & clothing business as "swan skins". Used to make powder puffs, swan skins became a standard trade article of the Hudson Bay Co. as early as 1772 and as late as 1903. As many as one thousand swans have been stripped of their breast skins and feathers on a single occasion. The carcasses were left to rot.

This big graceful bird was once near extinction. Now it has found sanctuary in several parks. In the thirties there were only sixty left in the United States, with only forty in Western Canada. The feather trade and wet land farming encroachment on their habitat had taken their toll. In 1935 Red Lakes Migratory Waterfowl Refuge began with a population of only fifty birds and by 1947 it had increased the number to two hundred and seven. Between 1951 to 1957 it stabilized at 500 with one hundred cygnets being born a year. Birds were transferred to Oregon, Nevada, South Dakota, Wyoming, and Manitoba with success. Now over 2,000 exist in the once depleted habitat. In all there are now perhaps eight to nine thousand in the wild, including two thousand mating pairs. For twenty years the Minnesota Parks System has also had a breeding program and is about to release swans in the wilderness, where as of yet there are none left where there used to be thousands. They are still in need of protection to assure their existence, but the turnaround of their decline has gone down in history as an early wildlife management success.

# SERENGETI

My Africa,
I am your offspring

The wind blows me the scents
Of your children.

The Cape Buffalo, Wildebeest,
Giraffe and Gazelle
Roam through your hair.

My eyes
Are your eyes.

The Serengeti plain
Blooms in colors
That are your reflection.

The sun brings life
And it parches
Your golden skin.

We your children
Wait for your tears
To fall on our faces.

So that we
Might sustain ourselves
For one more beat
Of your heart,

My Africa.

*John Ballou*

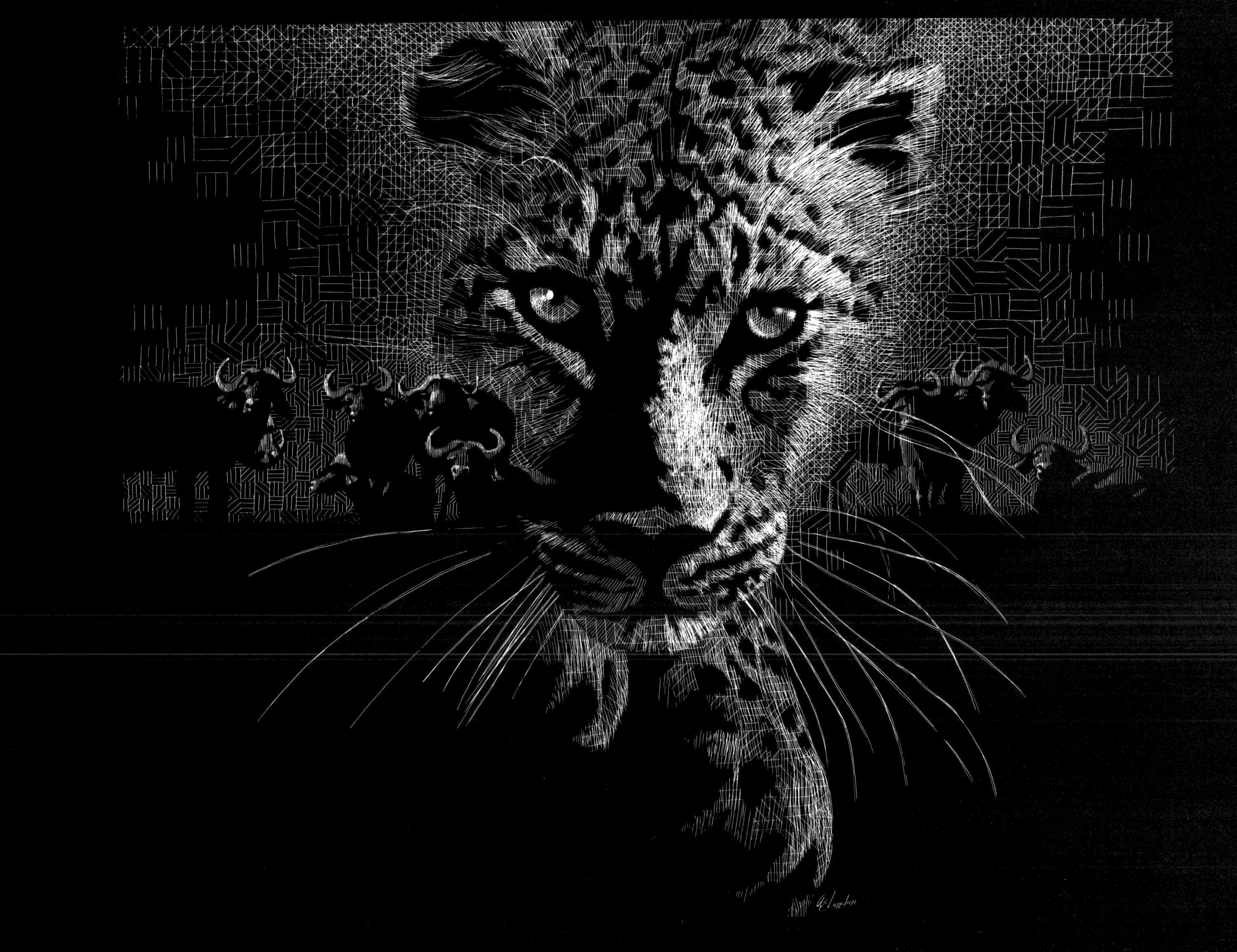

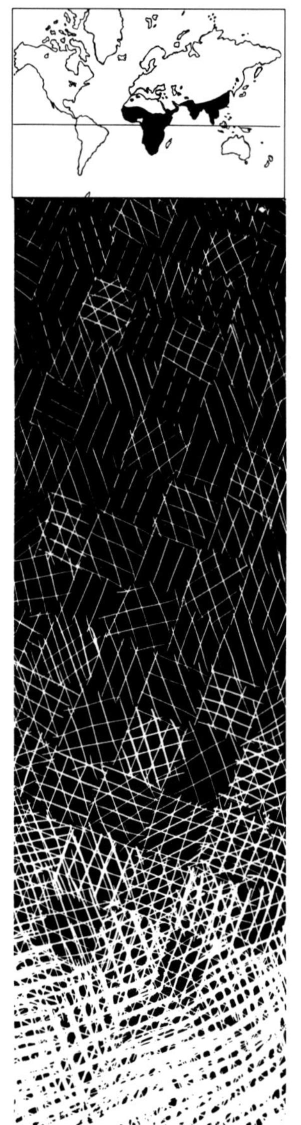

# *The Geographical Distribution of the Leopard*

The leopard is the most widespread member of the cat family. It is found in Africa south of the Sahara and in southern Asia, with scattered populations in North Africa, in Arabia, and in the Far East. They live in areas which have a reasonable supply of cover and prey animals. These areas include tropical rain forests, the arid savanna and cold mountainous regions almost to the edge of suburban populations.

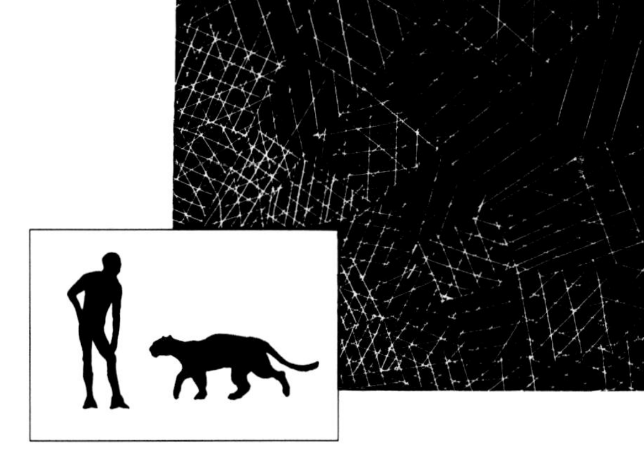

# LEOPARD

*(Panthera pardus)*

The leopard's adaptable hunting and feeding behavior has made it the most geographically widespread member of the cat family. The sleek cat catches a wide variety of prey—mainly small animals and birds. Using stealth and speed, the leopard stalks at close range and ambushes in a short fast rush. Usually leading a solitary existence, it does not compete with lions and tigers which pursue larger game. The edges of the female leopard territories overlap one another only on the edges, while the male territories overlap one another much more on a larger mosaic.

The cat's spots provide excellent camouflage, especially in trees. Its extremely sensitive and prominent whiskers are characteristic of nocturnal hunters who feel their way through the night. The black panther is a leopard with its recessive genes expressed as a black coat. It has been thought to be a separate species and has a mythology of its own, but the two are one and the same.

The leopard makes good use of trees. It rests safely aloft, shaded from the midday sun. From a tree top the leopard will survey the surroundings for prey and on occasion drop directly onto a passing animal. It also drags its kills up into the trees, where it can eat and store them out of reach of most scavengers.

The leopard's fur is highly prized by the wealthy to wear as clothing. Their pelts are coveted as trophies. Western sport hunters list them in their "Big Five" of most highly rated prey, a list which also includes the lion, the buffalo, the elephant, and the rhinoceros. Also, leopards are persecuted by farmers because of their attacks on livestock. This means that, though there are still well over one hundred thousand individuals surviving in isolated pockets of Asia and Africa in areas where the population pressure is low, the leopard's numbers are rapidly declining. This decline will further intensify as agriculture and further urbanization force other animals into the leopard's territory, escalating competition for game.

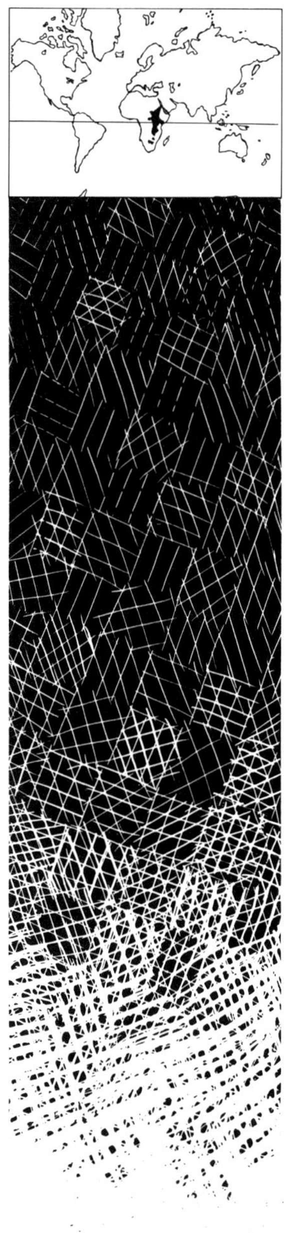

# *The Geographical Distribution of the Cape Buffalo*

The cape buffalo was once common throughout all of Africa south of the Sahara. Due to a disease from domestic cattle called Rinderpest, cape buffalo survive only in isolated populations in South and East Africa where the disease has not yet reached. There it lives in the savannas and woodlands. Its close relative, the forest buffalo, lives in the forests near the Equator.

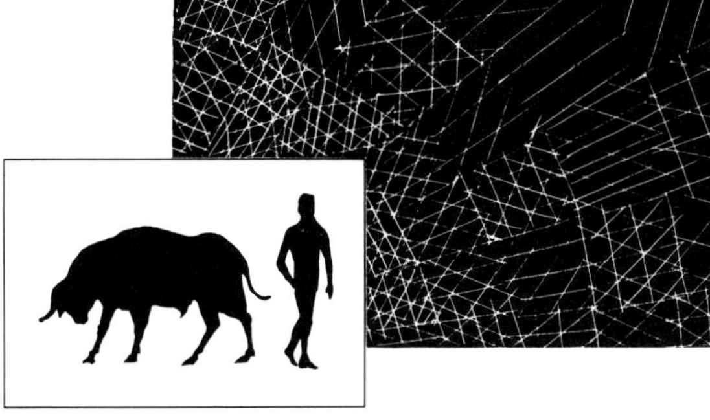

# CAPE BUFFALO

*(Syncerro caffer)*

The cape buffalo has the reputation as being the most dangerous of the African game animals. These ox-like creatures weigh nearly a ton and will charge full force in a blind panic at up to thirty five miles per hour. Even a heavy bore rifle may not stop but only incense them. Their thick powerful neck slows down the entry of the bullet. They have been known to trample and gore their victims until little that is recognizable remains. A herd will even pass its victim from one pair of horns to another until dead. The only defense from a charge is to climb a tree or to hide behind an immovable object.

Under peaceful circumstances the buffaloes are not aggressive. The lion, their only natural enemy, usually takes only the young or infirm. Never far from water, cape buffalo drink in early morning and evening, sometimes wallowing or splashing in the mud. Grass is the main staple of their diet, but leaves and twigs are acceptable alternatives. Like other grazers, their muzzle is flat and squared.

In the last century ecological changes in the culture of Africans, who are obsessed with raising large numbers of cattle, have infringed upon many wild animal feeding ranges. The result has been the overcrowding and killing off of large numbers of animals. Contracted directly from domesticated cattle, the disease Rinderpest has decimated most of the African population of buffalo, except in scattered locations where the disease has not reached. Herds once numbered up to two thousand, but now most groupings range from a few dozen to several hundred. This and increased urban population further affect the predators who depend upon them. Of course, the dangerous nature of the cape buffalo makes it a highly desired game prize, further imperiling its survival. Africa is slowly realizing the great loss it is experiencing as the result of its growth and modernization. Unfortunately this increasing awareness has been drastically slow. The only hope is that, as Africans struggle for economic stability, they will hear those of us who are concerned and will not forget to include the preservation of the qualities they were endowed with at birth— Nature itself.

# MERMAID AND MANATEES

In the weightlessness
Of liquid space
No landbound rules apply
To vision.

A trail of bubbles rises
As an exotic veil.
The absence
Of gravity's persistent weight
Is bliss.

Here, the smooth lines
Of sleek surfaced creatures
Are the standard
For grace.

*Bruce C. Eriksen*

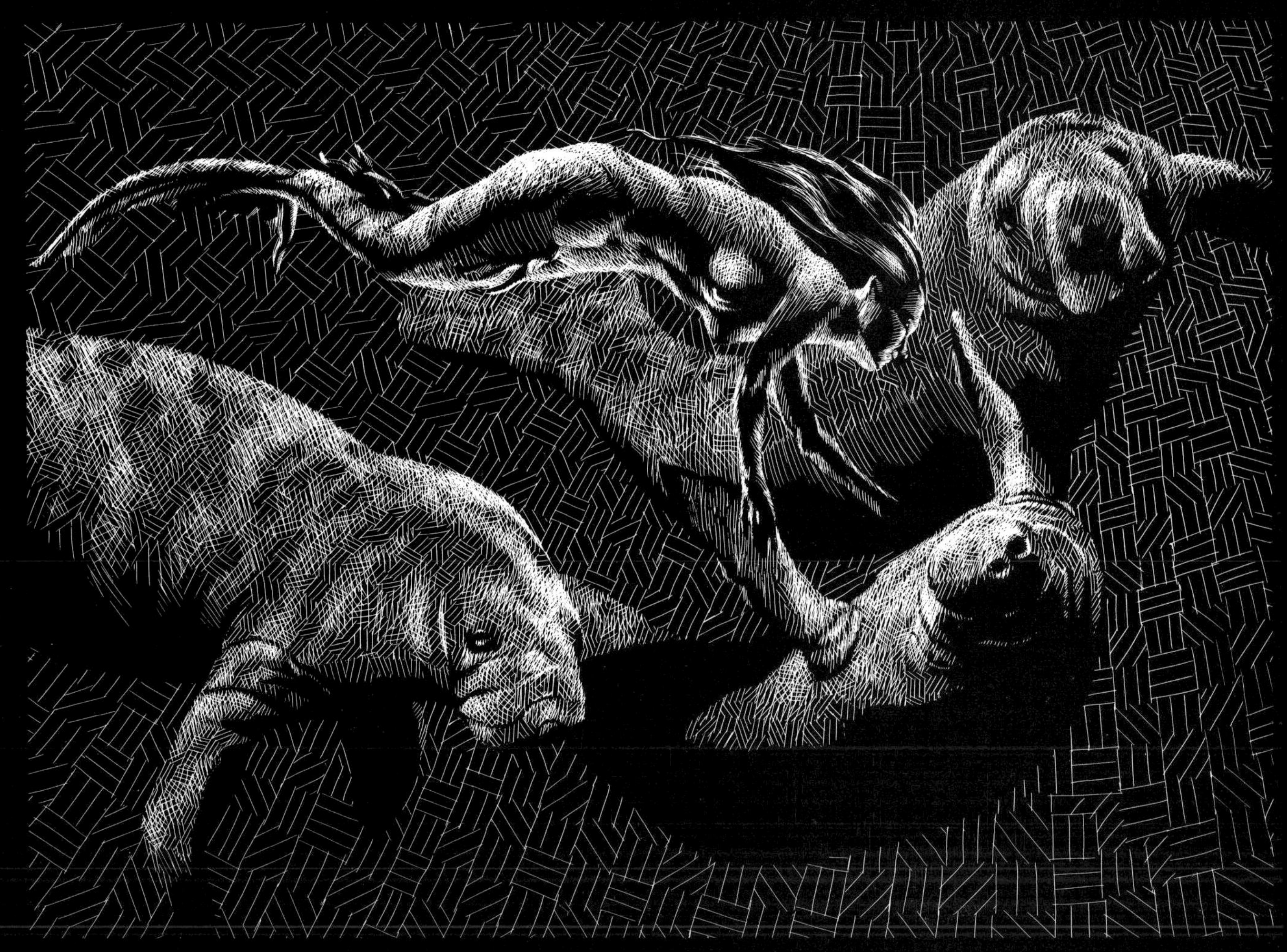

"Saw a strange creature swimming in St. Johns Harbour... strakes of hair down the neck... whether it were a mermaid or no, I know not; I leave it for others to judge."
*Eyewitness Account in the year 1610*

*by Richard Whitbourn*

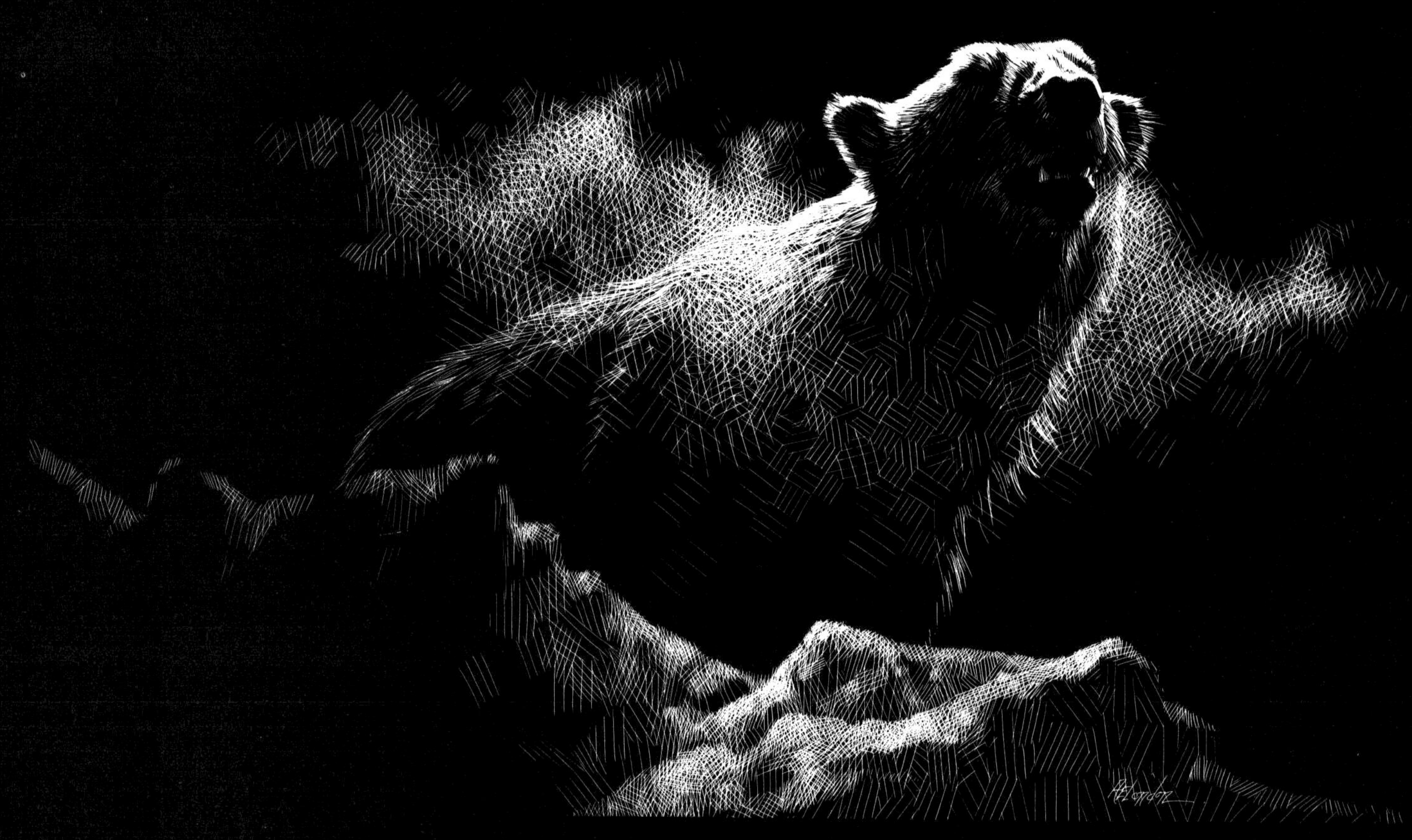

ON THE WIND

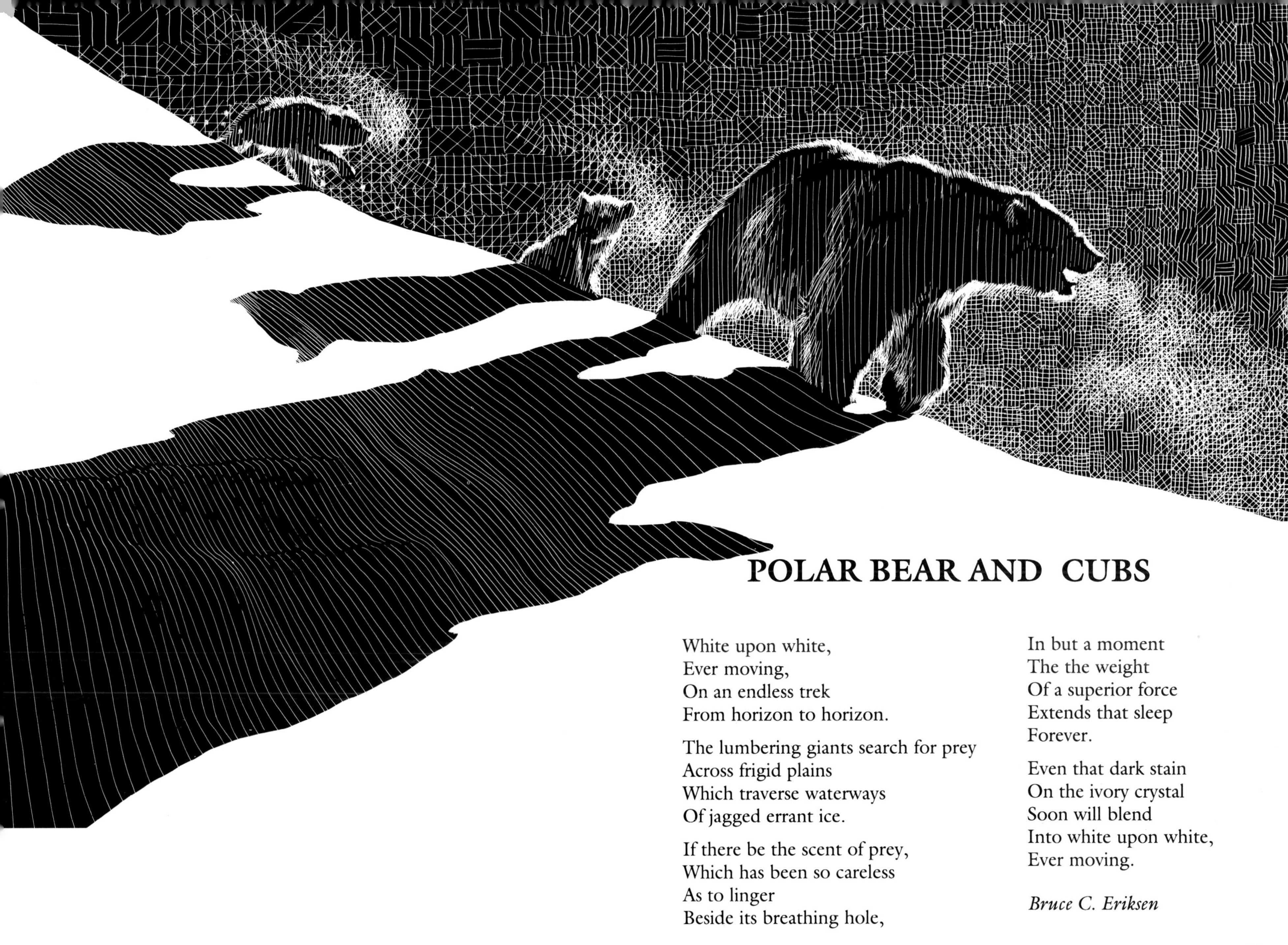

# POLAR BEAR AND CUBS

White upon white,
Ever moving,
On an endless trek
From horizon to horizon.

The lumbering giants search for prey
Across frigid plains
Which traverse waterways
Of jagged errant ice.

If there be the scent of prey,
Which has been so careless
As to linger
Beside its breathing hole,

In but a moment
The the weight
Of a superior force
Extends that sleep
Forever.

Even that dark stain
On the ivory crystal
Soon will blend
Into white upon white,
Ever moving.

*Bruce C. Eriksen*

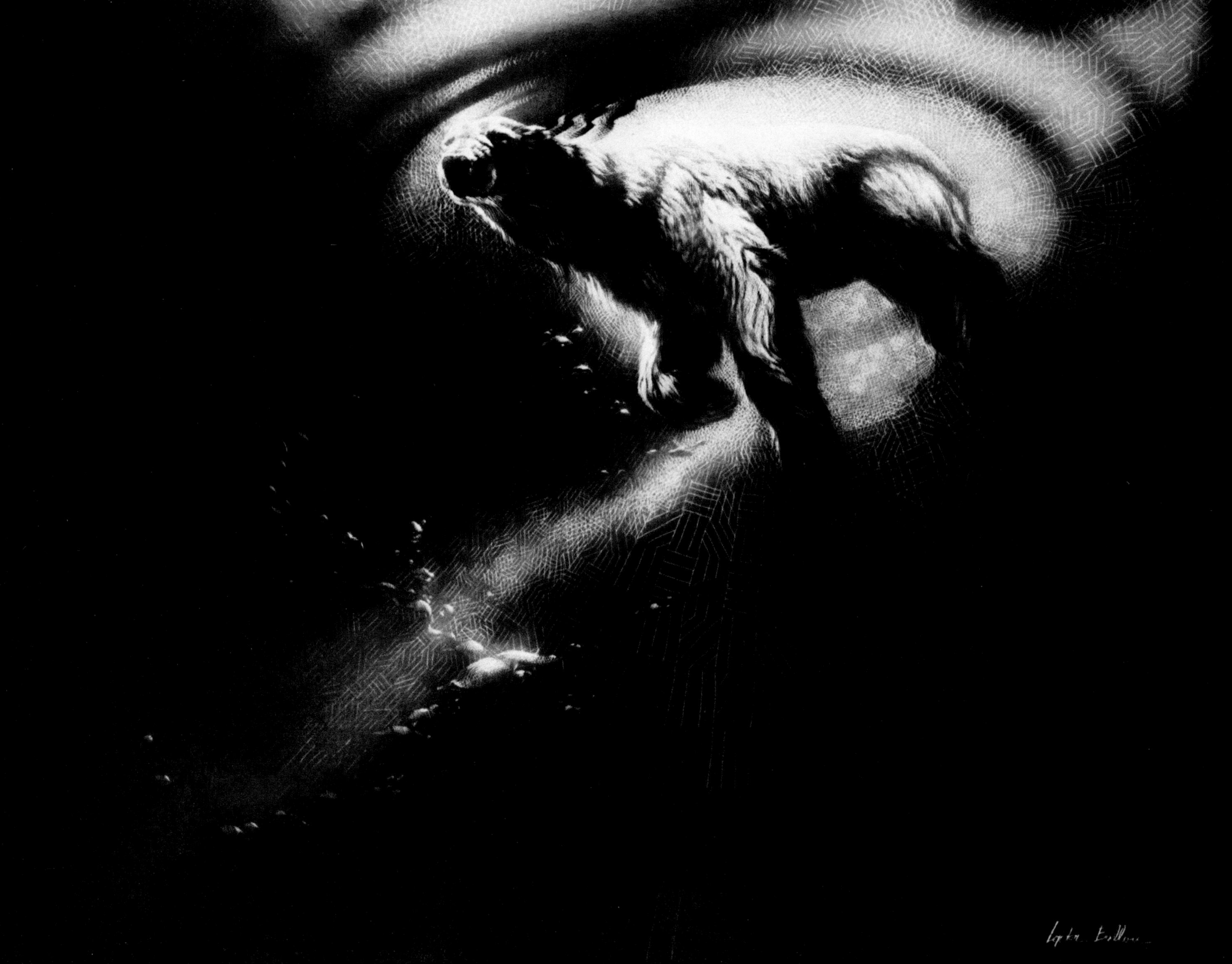

## THE ONE WHO FLIES

Deep down
In the cold blue,
It turned, rolled,
And glided,
Like a great bird.
It is no wonder
The Eskimo says
A bear can fly.

*Bruce C. Eriksen*

# THE ARCTIC FOX

Nestled
In your grey blue coat
Against the white
White arctic snow,
Your downy softness
Seems to beg
For the luxury
Of a caress.

But the alertness
In your eyes
Reminds us
That you are a wild thing
Who needs
The endless expanse
Of the polar plain
Where you may tag behind
In the tracks
Of the great white bear
With whom
You share destiny.

Knowing this,
We hope
That the human-like curiosity
Which endears you to our hearts
Will be tempered
Enough to spare you
The brutality
Of the trap
Or the humiliation
Of a cage,
Which would reduce you
To a commodity
Worn to satisfy
The blind greed
Of the vain.

Be quick
Be fast and silent
Be free

*Bruce C. Eriksen*

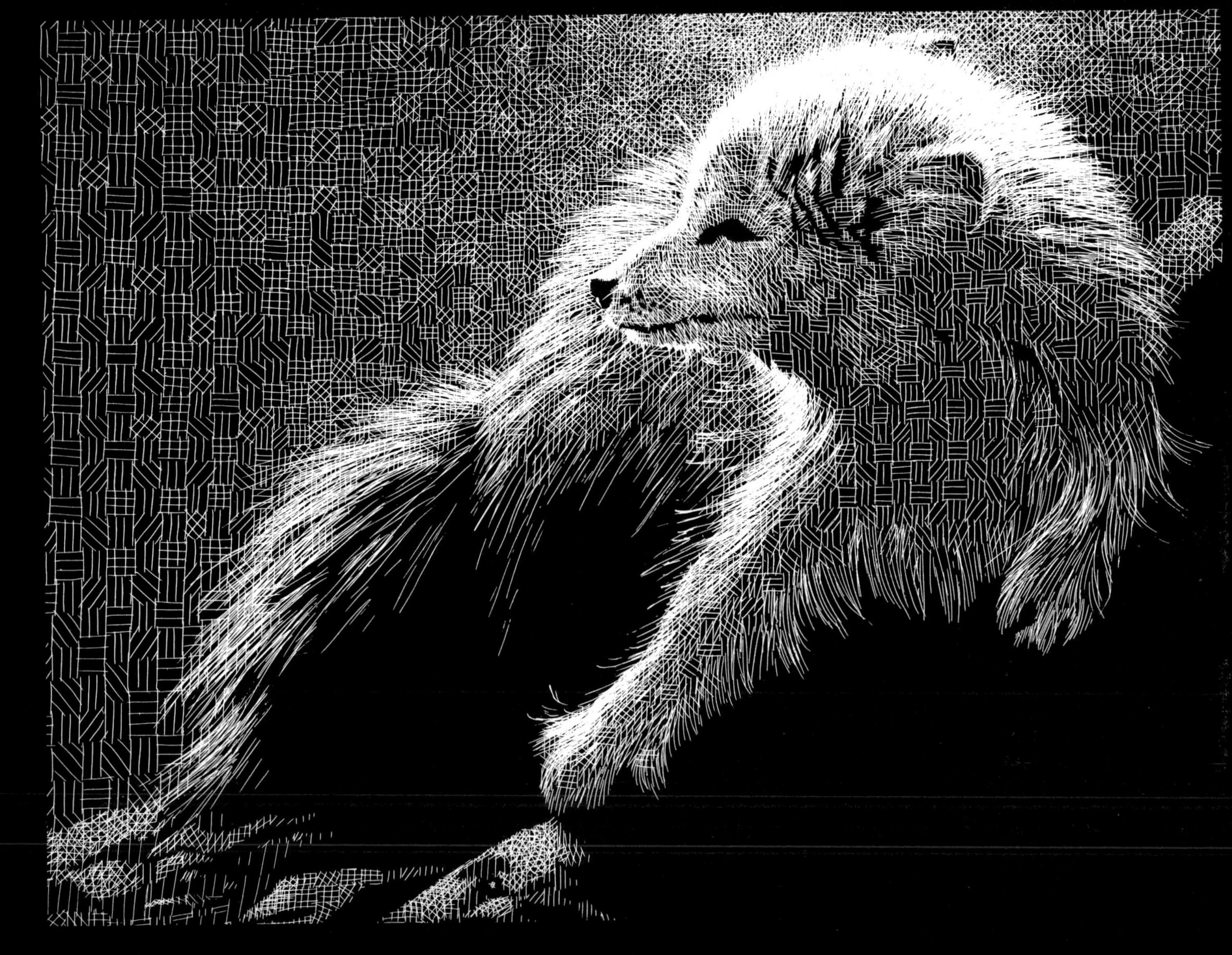

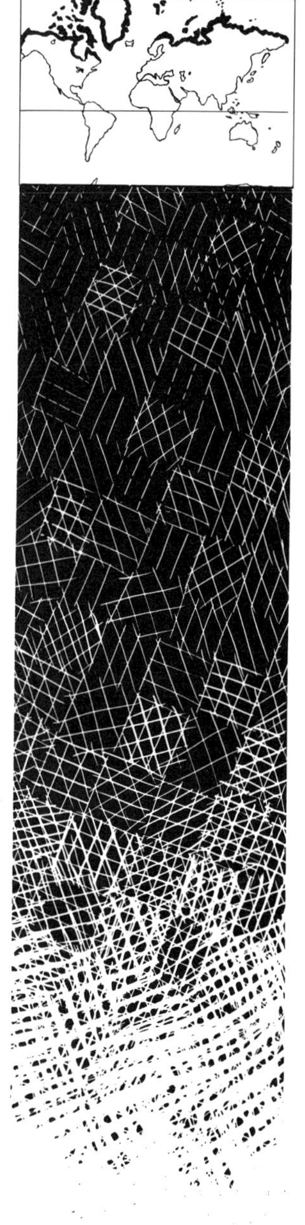

# *The Geographical Distribution of the Arctic Fox*

The home of the arctic fox is the arctic coast and islands, but every fourth winter it migrates southward. Occasionally it may reach northern Saskatchewan and Manitoba. The fox's range expands during the winter, following the polar bear's trail for leavings. Its usual range is circumpolar in the tundra latitudes, including islands of the polar sea, the coastal areas of Greenland, from northeastern Quebec to north of the tree limit of northwestern Alaska, south along the Bering Sea to the Alaska peninsula and onward to the Aleutian Islands.

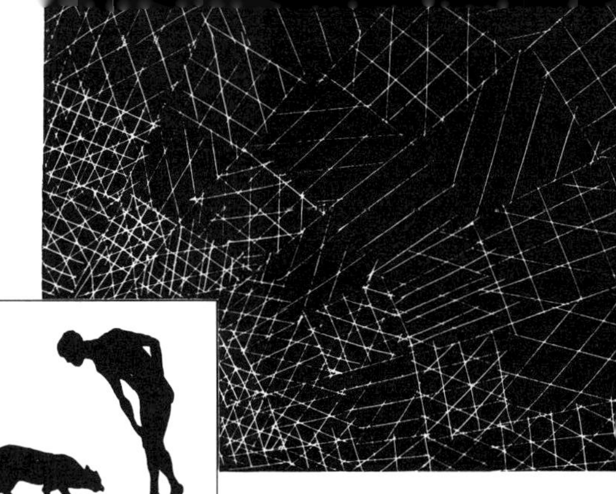

# ARCTIC FOX

*(Alopex lagopus)*

These small foxes have a remarkable tolerance to cold temperatures. Their metabolic rate does not increase until temperatures reach minus 50°c. They methodically forage to feed on sea birds, ptarmigans, shore invertebrates, fruits and berries, and carrion. In the abundant summer months they gorge themselves on small animals. They store surplus food by freezing it in holes dug in the ground, or hidden under rocks in anticipation of those times of scarcity. Often they are found in the company of polar bears in a jackal-like, scavenger role, cleaning up the remains of the giants' kills.

Ranging over a maximum of 2,100 to 15,000 acres, they mark conspicuous landmarks such as clumps of grass with feces and urine. Family groups are generally composed of one adult male and several vixen who communicate by scent and sound. They call out quite often as when an enemy approaches or during the breeding season.

The fox's insatiable curiosity and tameness towards humans makes it extremely vulnerable to capture. Its foraging practices also make it susceptible to contamination by toxic, polluted and diseased animals. Its coat varies in color depending upon the season, from pure white after shedding to blue grey in winter and to finally a darker color in the summer. The fur coat that works so well to keep it warm in extreme temperature is valued by furriers for its beautiful fluffy appearance and unusual coloring, especially in the rare blue-grey stage of middle winter.

Like ivory and the skins of other endangered species, the only place to admire the arctic fox pelt is on the animal in the wild. Perhaps there will be a day when all hunters aim cameras, not guns.

# SILVERBACK AND BABY

So much like us
We say,
Pretending
That it is you
Not we
Who are the beast.

We see it in your eyes—
By the way
You look in ours
As you hold your young,

We find in you,
A reminder
Of our past,
And marvel
How strong!

So we capture you—
Put you on display,
And marvel
At your spectacle.

We laugh
And judge you quaint,
Primitive;
All the while,
We cut your trees,
Your home,

And now
That you are rare,
You see
With those gorilla eyes.
The question,
Though perhaps too late,

How like you
Are we?

*Bruce C. Eriksen*

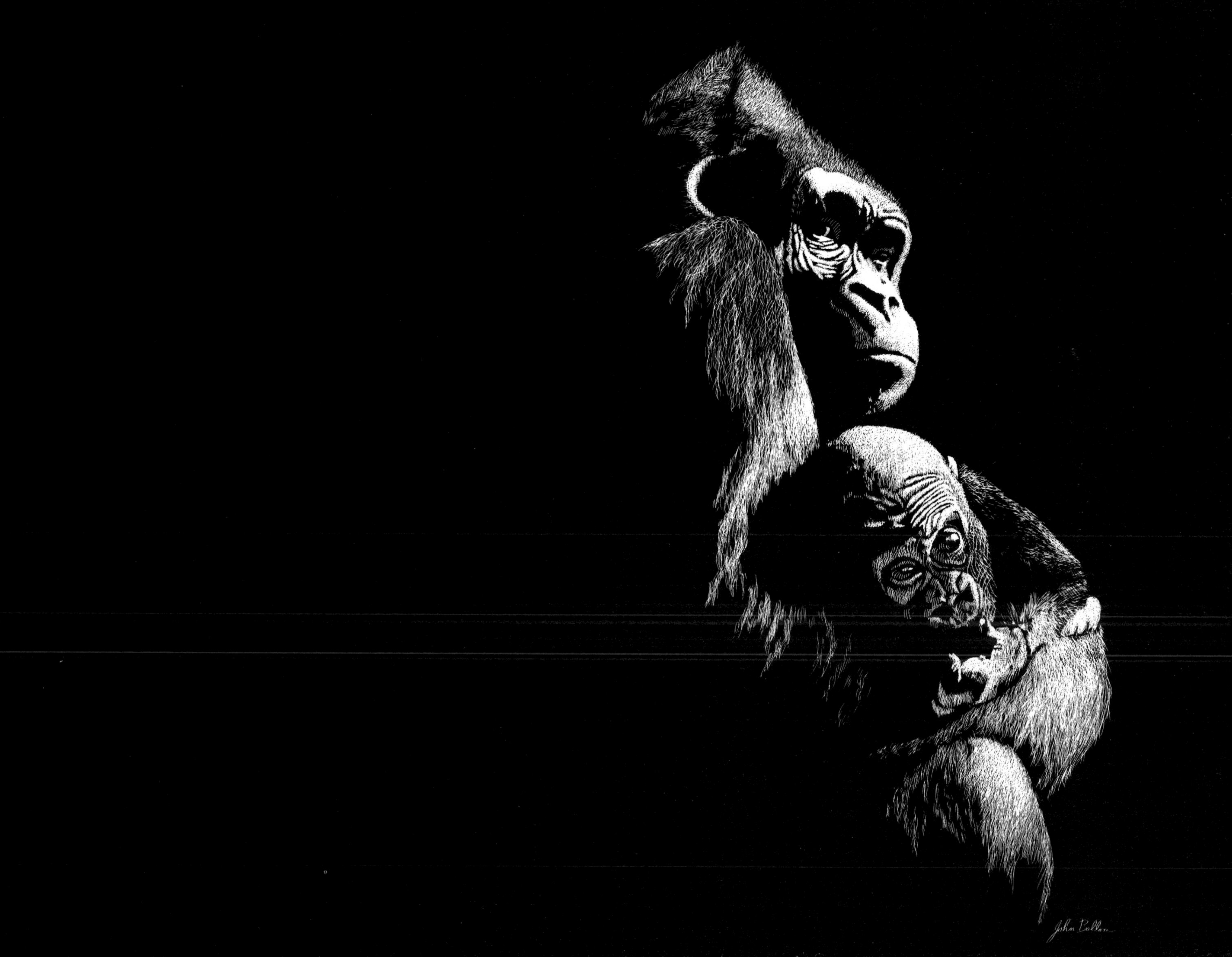

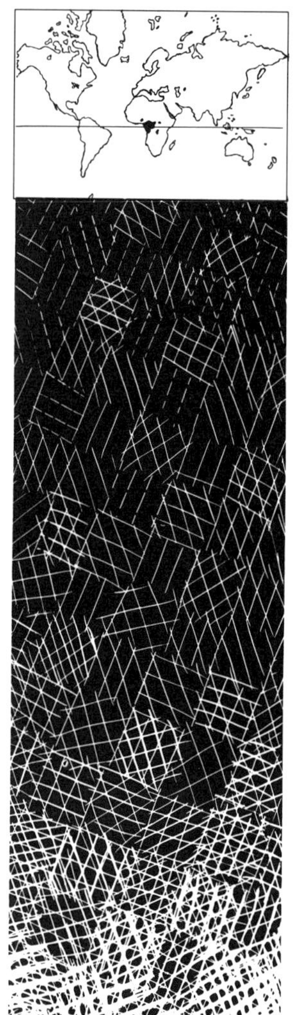

# *The Geographical Distribution of the Gorilla*

The gorilla lives in the central African secondary tropical forests. There are three races. The lowland gorilla (G.g. gorilla) ranges in Cameroon, Central African Republic, Gabon, Congo, and Equatorial Guinea. The eastern gorilla (G.g. graueri) is in East Zaire. The mountain gorilla (G.g. beringei) lives in Zaire, Rwanda, and Uganda at altitudes of about 5,450 to 12,500 feet.

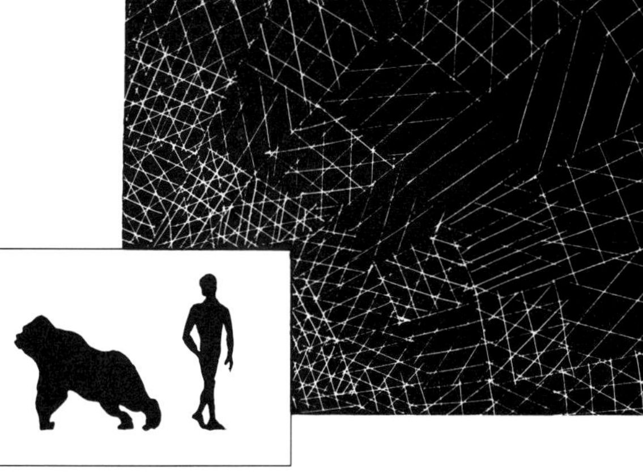

# GORILLA

*(Gorilla gorilla)*

Gorillas are the largest primate. They attain the weight of 300 to 400 pounds, grow as tall as 5 feet 9 inches, and often live 35 years in the wild, or up to 50 years in captivity. They are the closest relation in the animal kingdom to man, along with two species of chimpanzee. When left alone, they are gentle creatures that live in relatively permanent groupings and range within areas of 2 to 12 miles. Though they do eat fruit and occasionally meat, they are usually occupied with gathering their diet of leaves and stems.

Gorillas only show dangerously aggressive behavior in defense of their breeding rights or family groups. Those groups are usually composed of about 5 to 10 members but can be as large as 35. Their social interaction and communication skills are among the most sophisticated in the animal kingdom. In captivity they have even been taught to use the sign language used by the hearing impaired. Some gorilla intelligence quotients have been measured as high as 96. That makes these primates the most intelligent species on earth excluding man and perhaps the whale.

The gorillas' only threat in the wild is man. Their population, which was estimated in 1980 to be only 1,300 (only 365 mountain gorillas), has been in rapid decline. Their habitat is disappearing at an ever increasing rate. The forests gorillas depend upon are being cut down for timber, cleared for agriculture, and developed for industry. Gorillas used to exist in Nigeria but now their habitat is covered by cattle ranches. No small threat to their survival in the wild are commercial hunters who acquire them at the request of zoos.

Through the magic of film, naturalists are able to present to us glimpses of the gorilla in the isolation of their Garden of Eden. This is perhaps our last. As Africa politically awakens, it is first addressing the cultural problems of its peoples' displaced struggle for identity. The gorilla and many other species, who are also being displaced, have little chance to compete without human benefactors. If we are to express our "superior" intelligence, would it not be appropriate to protect the citizen of our planet who is the closest to us both in evolution and intelligence? Would it not establish and confirm the dignity of both and the sanctity of the bond of all life?

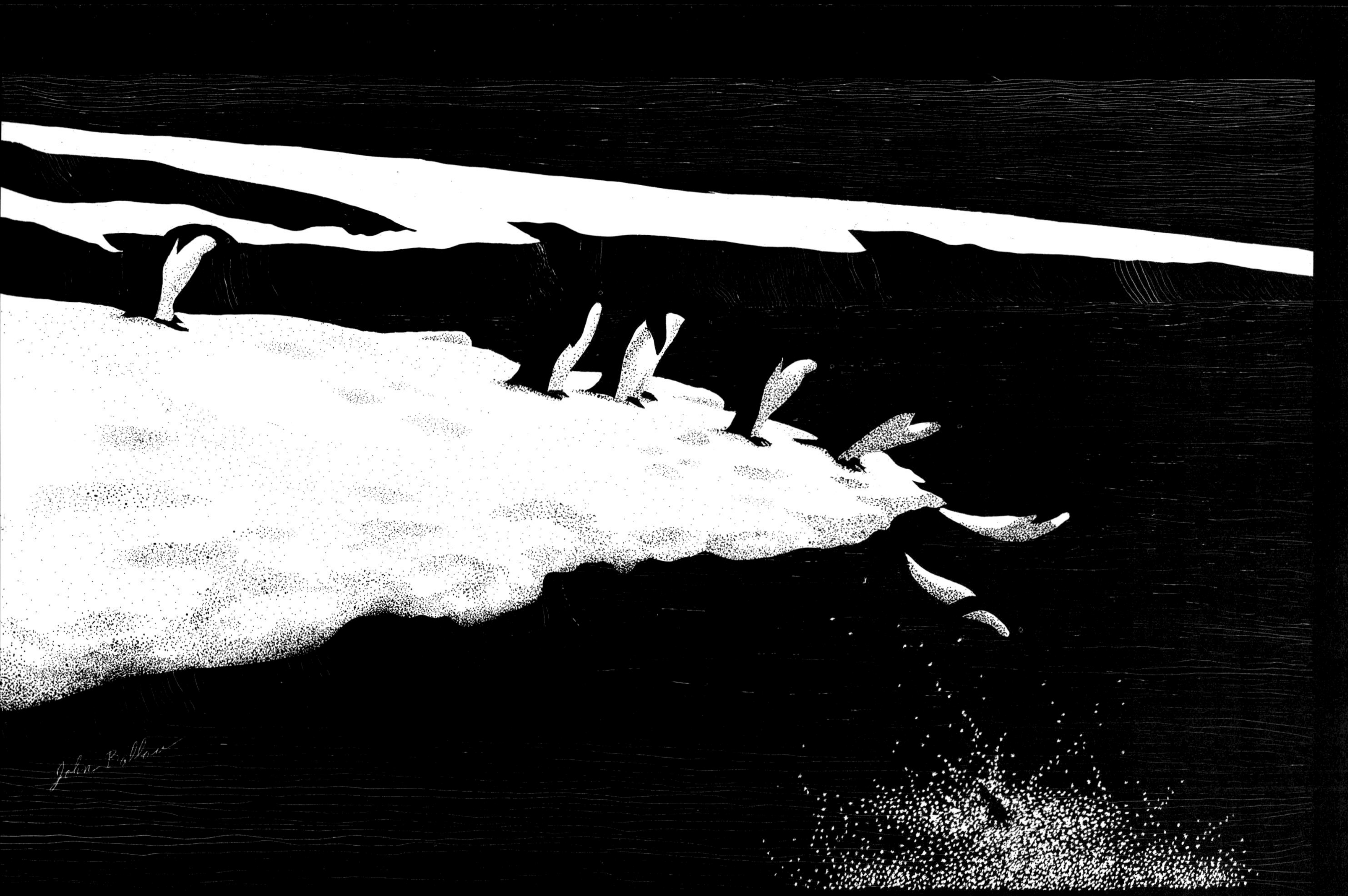

## PENGUINS

Like so many politicians
They assemble
On the icy edge.

The water is frigid,
But survival,
Their obsession,
Has evolved
Thick layers
Which insulate

Against all odds
In a world
Alien
To those of us
Who thrive
In the temperate zone.

They line up
In organized chaos
Not hesitating
To plunge
Into icy brine.

Now free
From the bounds of land,
And finally immersed
In the caldron
From whence they evolved,
The other extreme
Becomes...bliss.

*Bruce C. Eriksen*

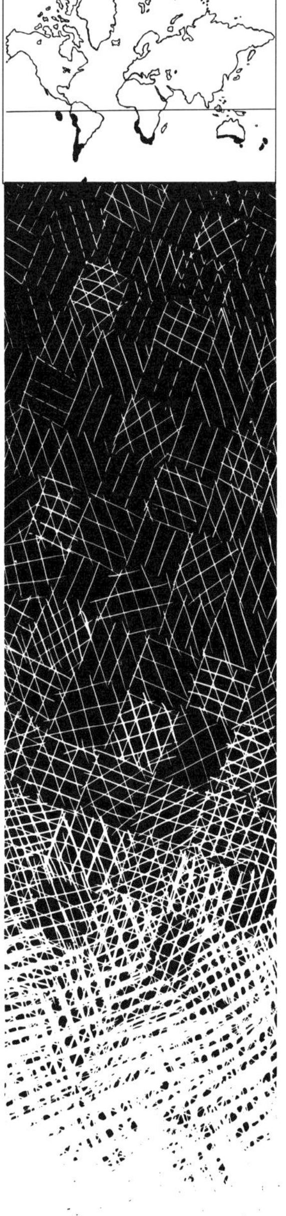

# *The Geographical Distribution of the Penguin*

Penguins are found in the Antarctic, New Zealand, South Australia, South Africa, South America, north to Peru and the Galapagos Islands. They live in habitats of sea water, ice, and rock on islands and coasts. They breed in habitats ranging from the bare lava shores of equatorial islands to sandy subtropical beaches, from cool temperate forests and subantarctic grass lands to antarctic sea ice.

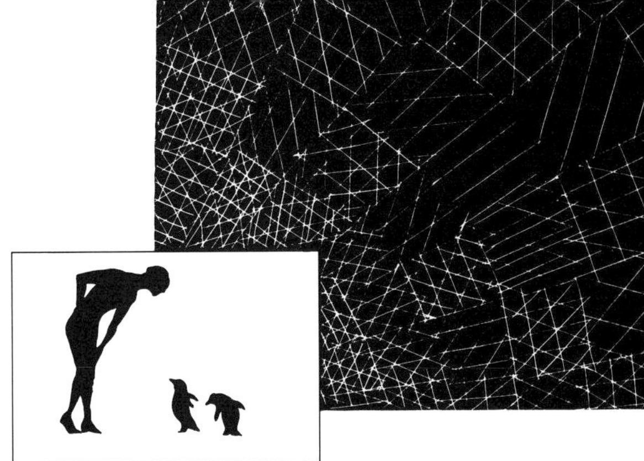

# PENGUINS

*(Pygoscelis adeliae)*

The penguin's only true flight is its dive into the water. Its ancestors must have opted to perfect underwater flight and paid for their new skills in doing so by losing the ability to do so above water. The penguin's flipper is not a modified arm but a modified wing. They are better adapted for life in the sea than any other group of birds. Densely covered by three layers of short feathers, the capacity for storing substantial fat reserves, and a highly developed "heat exchange system" of blood vessels in their large flippers and short legs combine with their streamlined shape to create efficient cold water swimmers. They insulate themselves from the cold via air trapped under their feathers. An additional ability to expel air from their feathers while diving to reduce buoyancy causes trails of bubbles as they descend. This further increases their ability to dive deep in search of prey. The main prey of penguins are crustaceans, fish, and squid, which they chase, catch, and swallow underwater.

Penguins have extremely interesting breeding and nesting practices. Each species has developed variations on the theme according to its nesting place and its particular adaptation. For example, the Gentoo penguins breed a little ways inland and must do much walking in the process of carrying nesting materials and food to their nests. The Magellanic penguins at Punto Argentina gather in rookeries and lay their eggs in sandy burrows. The large Emperor penguins hatch their eggs in the most severe conditions of a short summer and extreme cold. The males will gather in groups as large as 6,000 strong and huddle together when incubating their eggs. When they hatch they must be protected in the pouch-like folds of skin near their feet. They are fattened quickly and grow to as much as 28 pounds before the onset of winter.

Three species of penguins are presently endangered. The Galapagos penguins, with a total population of about 5,000 pairs, breed on only two islands in the Galapagos Archipelago. On one island they are seriously threatened by the presence of wild feral dogs. Yellow-eyed penguins have declined to fewer than five thousand pairs, because of changing patterns of land use and other disturbances to the coastal dune systems of New Zealand where they breed. Both the Jackass and Humbolt penguins occur in highly productive oceanic systems of nutrients that support large fishing industries. These populations have decreased alarmingly due to egg removal during guano collection. More recently, competition with fishermen for anchovies and pilchards has exerted pressure on their survival. All penguins are highly vulnerable to oil pollution. For instance, many Jackass penguins near the tanker route in the Straits of Magellan have died in oil incidents. Even the extremities of the earth are not exempt from the radical influence of humans. In fact the delicate balance of life in the sea is as easily polluted as the delicate taste of a gourmet soup. The sea, after all, is the soup stock and source of life.

# MAKING THUNDER

Ancient feathered cloud,
Unfurled wing,
Reach out and gather the sky.
Wet touch of the wind,
Lift the whales from the sea.
Eyes flash with light,
The waters thunder,
As the giants fall from the sky.
Thunderbird,
Gather our spirits.

*Northwest Indian Folk Lore*

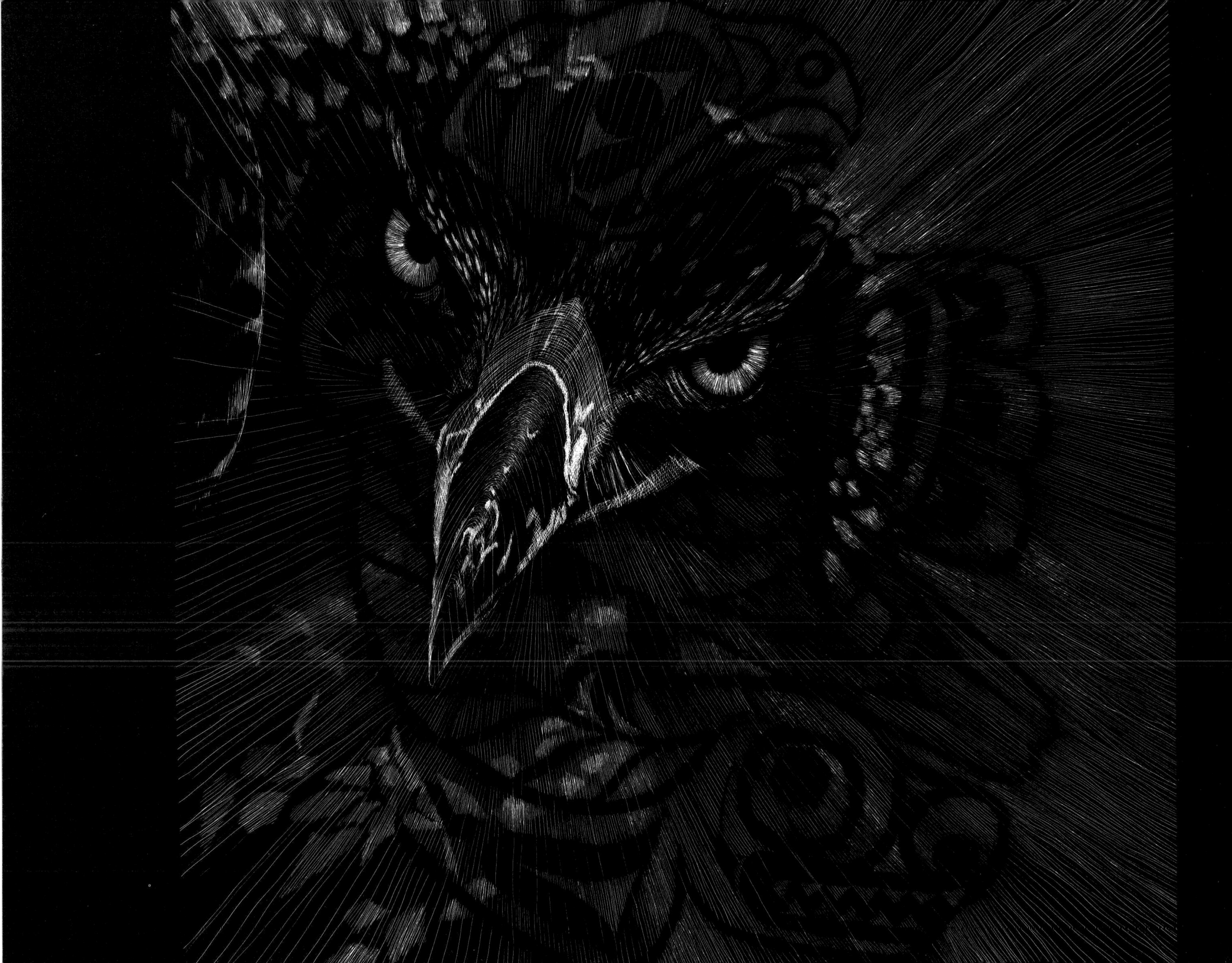

## TIGER LILIES

Silent
Articulated muscle
Pushes through
The dense stalks
And lush reeds
To where green pads float
On a reflecting pool,
Cooler
Than the paths
Which steam
In the mid-afternoon.

Too hot...
Better to yawn
And stretch,
Then settle
Into the velvet calm
Of still water.

Only the fragile scent
Of soft petalled lilies
Fills the humid air.

*Bruce C. Eriksen*

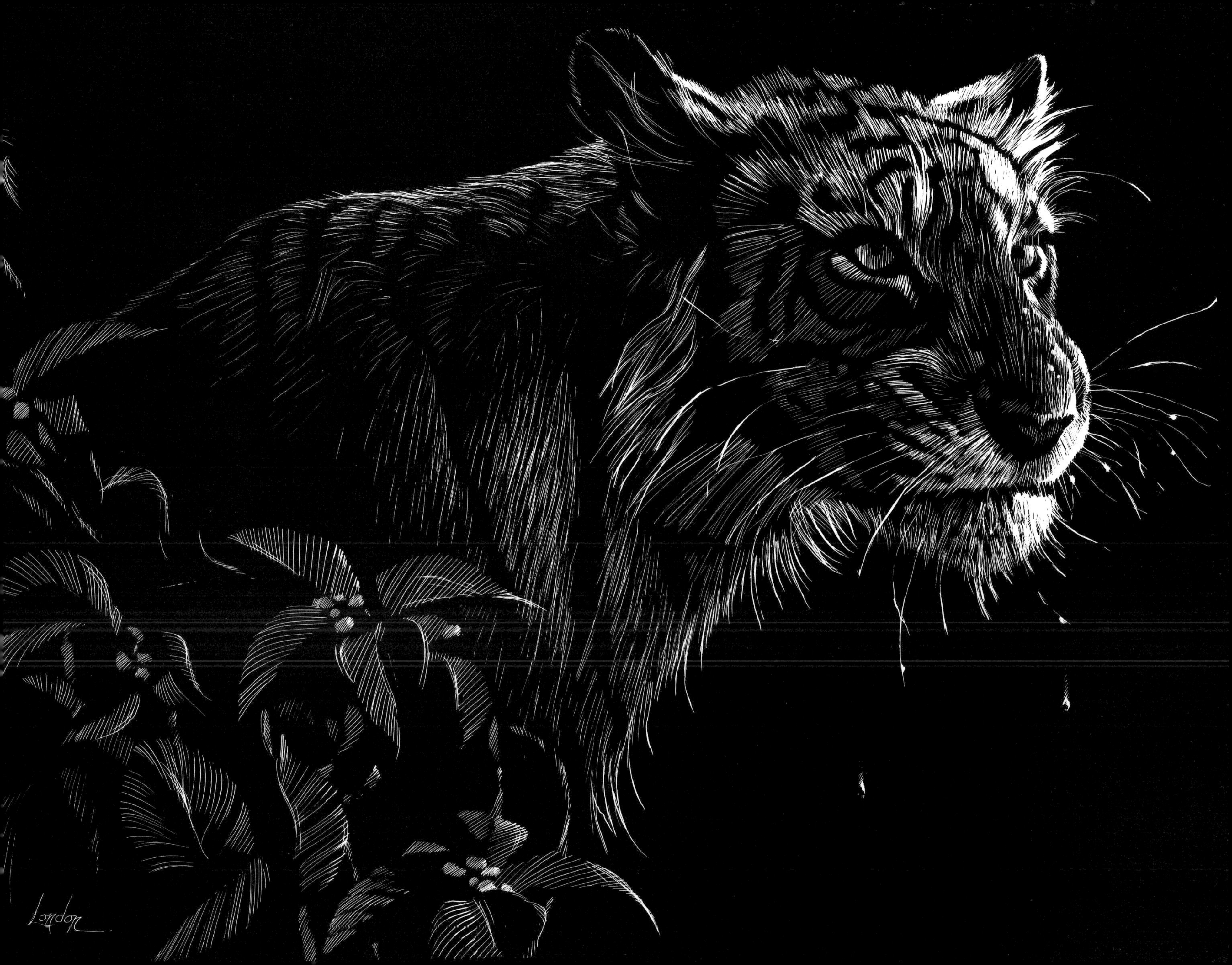

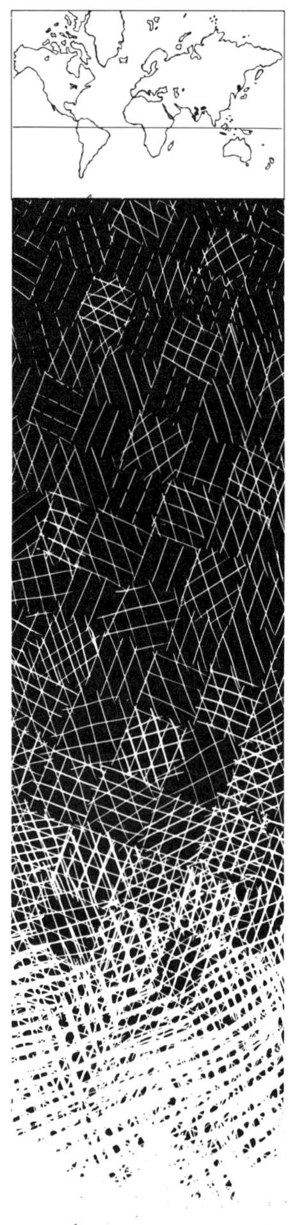

# *The Geographical Distribution of the Tiger*

The tiger used to range over most of Asia, China, and as far east as Turkey and as far north as North Korea, but now it is limited to India, Nepal, Bhutan, parts of Southeast Asia and Sumatra. Of the eight species of tiger (two may be entirely extinct), the larger and cold climate tigers, such as the Siberian, have been found at altitudes as high as 13,000 feet and in temperatures as low as -30 degrees. The smaller, warm climate tigers such as the Sumatran thrive in hot humid temperatures at lower elevations.

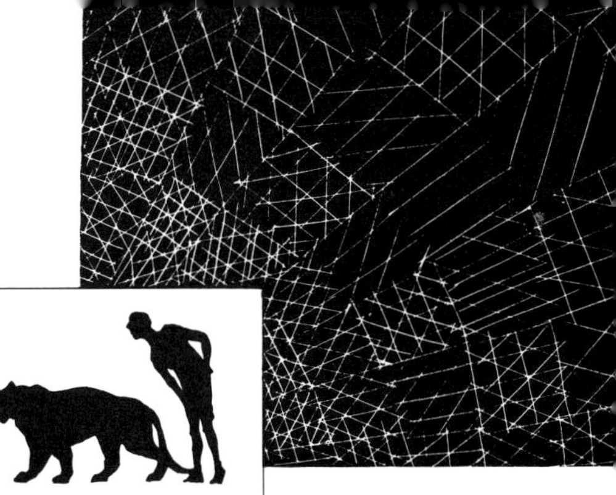

# TIGER

*(Panthera tigris)*

The tiger is the largest known cat alive today. It can grow as long as 13 feet and as large as 450 fifty pounds. Some have been reported to over 700 pounds. This great cat leads a solitary existence, usually hunts alone at night, and prefers to stay out of sight. It will normally run and seek cover when discovered, rather than attack. The tiger's sense of smell is poor so it depends on its more acute senses of hearing and sight to hunt. It is usually found near a water course where it hunts, bathes and enjoys swimming.

Although deer and pigs are the mainstay of its diet, the tiger eats a wide variety of food as small and as diverse as crabs, turtles, and fish, and as large as young elephants or rhinoceroses weighing over 1,000 lbs. Its strength is as incredible as its appetite. It will carry the carcass of an animal more than twice its own weight long distances in order to hide it. There the tiger may feast on it for days at a time.

The tiger is considered to be more dangerous than the lion because it is more powerful and ferocious when provoked. Instances of man killing have created the reputation of "man eater". In almost every case, such behavior has been proven to have been caused by tigers who were wounded, weakened or too old to procure their normal game in an area continually pressured by human settlement. Such mishaps often provoked the fervor of the local authorities to protect villagers. The myths that may arise from these tragic events also entice the zealousness of big game hunters who consider the most dangerous and magnificent game as the most desirable of trophies. The result has been overkill. In 1973 the total population of tigers had been reduced from over 100,000 to fewer than 4,000, a reduction of 96%. Project Tiger, begun in 1973, convinced governments to cooperate in their preservation and now the population is nearer 7,500 individuals worldwide.

The encroachment upon the tigers' hunting ground by human urbanization, agriculture and the zealousness of the big game hunter has been enough to destabilize their population, but perhaps the most underrated threats to the tiger are the apothecaries and pseudo-medical herbalists and healers that abound in eastern society. The bones, blood, heart, flesh, fangs, and genitals are believed to have magical therapeutic value, thus raising the tigers' black market value. This unfortunate superstition is decimating their already dwindled population. The misconception that the powerful magnificence of a creature like the tiger can be bought, borrowed, or stolen dies too slow a death in a world where people desire imaginary quick cures to their personal ailments and shortcomings. It is most unfortunate that tigers are dying daily as a sacrifice to these backward and false beliefs.

# THE BATHING ELEPHANT
## (In the Current of the Moon's Rays)

Today,
In this pause
From my own frenzied pace,
I watch you.

Spraying away the day's heat,
Wearing your centuries' old smile,
Bathing in the current of the moon's rays,
Swaying to the rhythms of your ballet,

I see how deliberately you move,
Articulating your immense mass
In the myriad of subtle movements
That are you.

In this moment,
When the day's quest for sustenance
Has been replaced
By a moment of refreshment,
I must restrain my desire to intrude.

You must have your privacy,
And this moment of restoration,
For the day grows short.

You will need your stamina,
Your strength and your wisdom,
Because the rigors of today
Are but a taste of the task
That lies before you
Tomorrow.

*Bruce C. Eriksen*

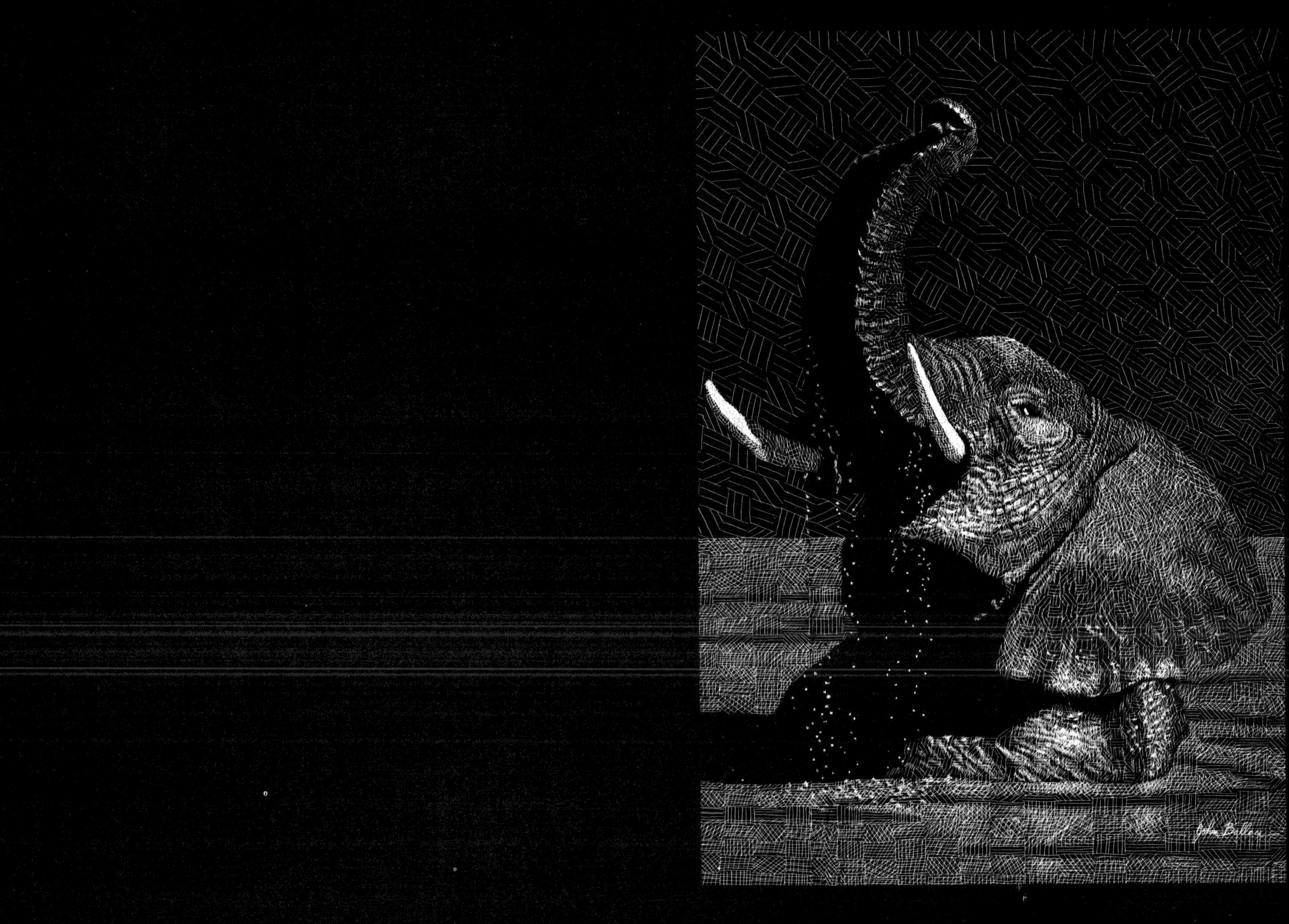

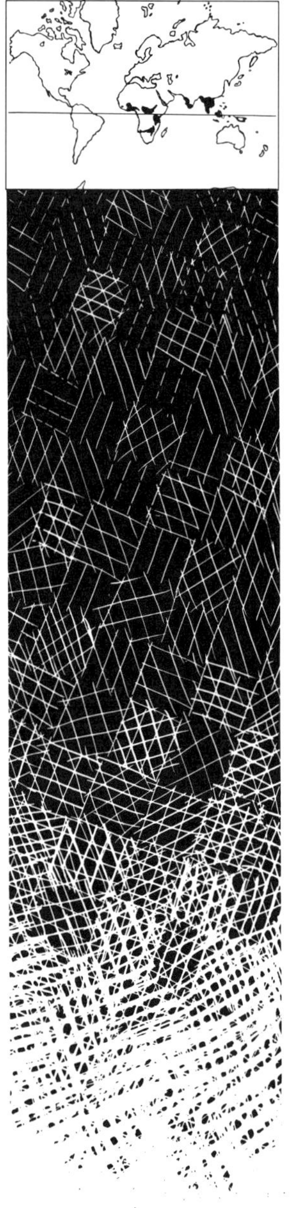

# *The Geographical Distribution of the African Elephant*

The African elephant used to be found throughout the African continent, south of the Sahara, on the Savanna and in the forests. To satisfy the large appetite, which serves to maintain its tremendous size, an elephant will travel as far as thirty kilometers at a time to find better vegetation and water sources, therefore requiring extensive grazing range. Those ranges are now greatly reduced as the result of expanding agriculture and political boundaries. The subspecies Savanna, or bush elephant, lives on the plains in eastern, central and southern zones, while the subspecies, the forest elephant, is now mainly restricted to the Addo National Park in South Africa.

# AFRICAN ELEPHANT

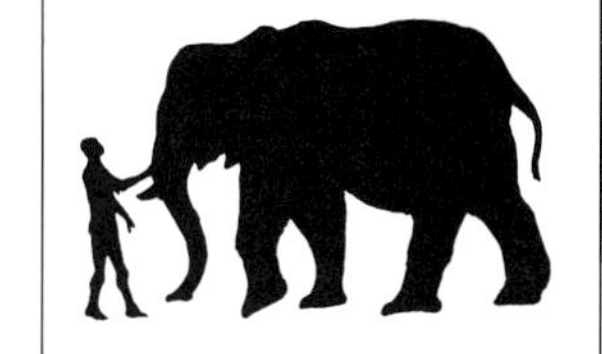

*(Loxodonta africana)*

Because the elephant is the largest land dwelling animal on earth it has evolved fascinating adaptations. The trunk is an elongated nose and upper lip which allows the huge animal to reach the ground. It is strong enough to uproot trees but sensitive enough to pick up very small objects. The elephant also uses the trunk to drink, bathe, squirt, caress, threaten, and even to snorkel underwater. The thick pillar-like legs of the elephant are supported by feet which distribute the weight of each step so flatly and evenly that they leave hardly a track. The large surface area of its wing-like ears with their flapping movement ventilates the blood which courses through the massive bulk and lengthy circulatory system.

The elephant's size also affects its eating habits. In the wet season it eats large amounts of grasses and an assortment of leaves from the moist parts of trees and shrubs. The elephant's digestive system allows it to turn to the less nutritious, woody parts of trees and shrubs through droughts. As much as 330 pounds of food are passed through the body, half of it left undigested. The elephant requires 19 to 20 gallons of water a day and will travel 30 kilometers if it has "sniffed the wind" for a rain-stimulated growth of eatable shrubs.

They are extremely sociable and live in family units. The older, matriarchal females pass on their considerable learned experience, such as knowledge of water sources, food supplies, and ways of avoiding danger to the younger members. For example, bush pilots have observed elephants cluster in a tight group to cover the tusks of their elders so as to avoid being hunted for ivory.

As the range of the elephant is limited by human competition for land cultivation, cattle grazing, and political boundaries, the very adaptations which supported the elephant's size so well in the unfettered wild may now be its undoing. Government sponsored culling practices are touted as a means to limit the number of the herd so that the rest will not starve. However, many conservationists protest that many governments have gone too far. Culling is linked to a trade of elephant products which has become such a profitable "managed income" that governments are reluctant to give it up. Extensive poaching further complicates the problem. The trade in elephant by-products is seductive to those only interested in high profit. 50,000 to 150,000 elephants are being killed each year. The elephants' breeding habits make it next to impossible for zoos to breed them, thus further thinning the wild population.

The elephant has long been of value to man for its ability to learn to cooperate and for its agility and great strength. Because the elephant's ivory portends easy marketability, hunters have legally and illegally exploited it to the extent of the elephant's near extinction. Once again, the fate of these most magnificent of creatures lies in human hands. Compassion must be cultivated, while restraint and active conservation must be consistently enforced, or the elephant will not survive.

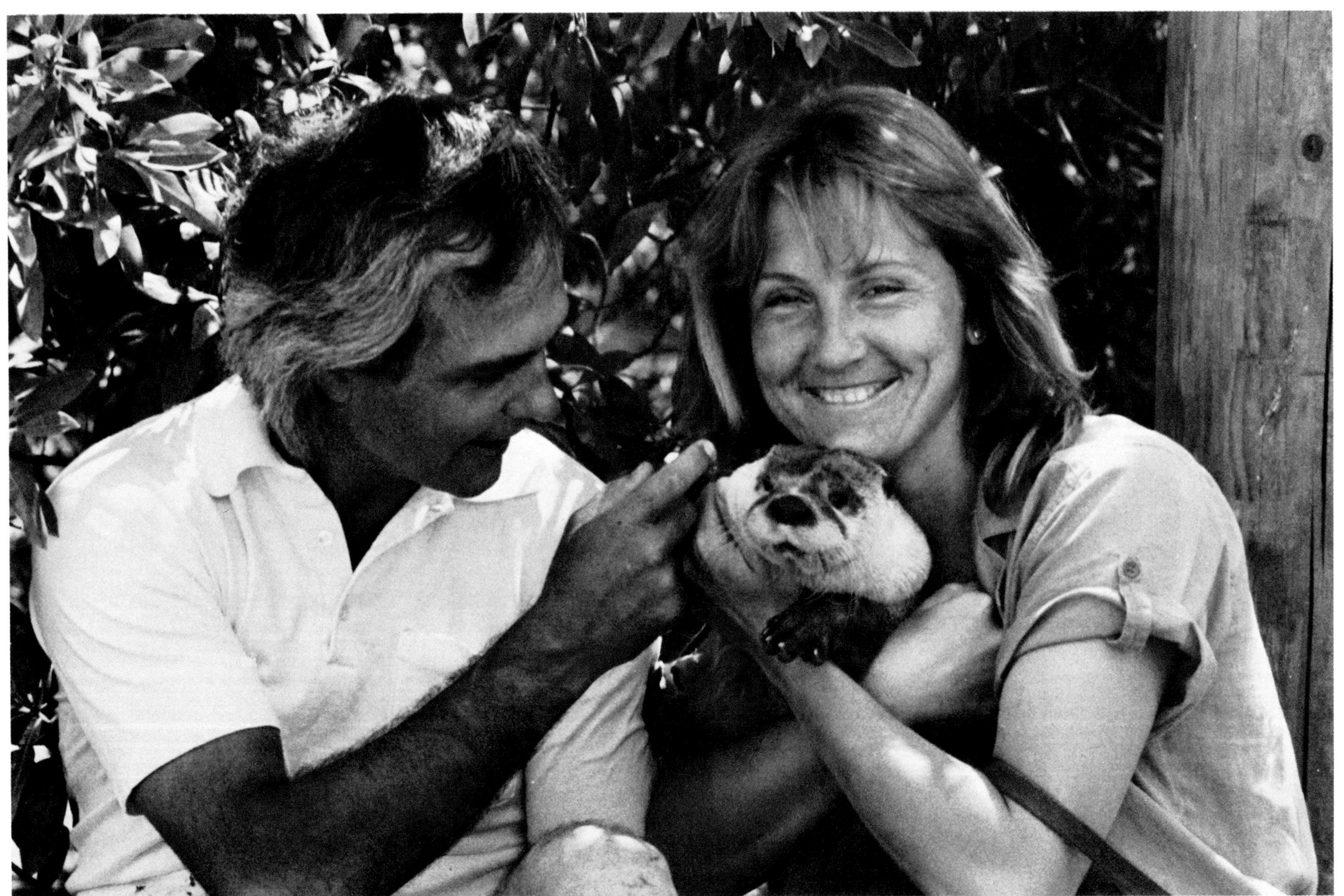

# About the Artists

When Anne London and John Ballou met six years ago at an art exhibition they immediately discovered that they had many common interests. He was an architect, she an illustrator, and both were painters. They also shared a great passion for the wilderness and its inhabitants. They both wished to create a project which would have a positive impact upon the environment. This mutual fascination and sense of purpose led to the beginning of their artistic collaboration. They now share a studio in Benicia at the mouth of the Sacramento waterway and the northernmost tip of the San Francisco Bay.

In their art, Anne London and John Ballou place the observer in the environment as a fellow creature who shares a particular niche, rather than as an intruder looking in from the outside. To accomplish this, they pay great attention to lighting and mood, seeking to inspire a feeling of empathy rather than sympathy for the animals.

For this wildlife series they have mastered the ancient art of intaglio etching, an especially appropriate medium for their depictions. With engraving tools they skillfully render a web of intricate patterns. On the surfaces of ink they have carefully applied, they delicately etch the dark surface away, exposing lighter layers of white clay. This requires intense concentration since there is no turning back once a mistake is made. The process is repeated over and over again through layer after layer of progressively lighter shades of prepared surface. This process affords the subtlety of tone and value they demand in the perfect execution of their art form. The unlimited dynamics of texture and brilliance which emerge from this technique allows them to go beyond mere representation to express the emotion they feel for their subjects.

Because they have willingly donated much of their work and time to marine biologists and researchers, these scientists in return have enthusiastically invited them to use their facilities as resources for firsthand observations. John and Anne like to spend as much time as possible in direct contact with the animals, playing with them and sharing the close proximity of their habitat. This adds a special depth and intimacy to their images. Such authenticity is a hallmark of their work which is often on exhibit within the same wildlife facilities.

Because of his background as an architect and unique understanding of the aesthetics of marine mammal environment, John has consulted on tank designs for the new home of Marine World/Africa U.S.A. in Vallejo, California. He believes tanks should be three-dimensional works of art designed first of all for the dolphin's comfort and enjoyment. After all, it is the home of highly intelligent individuals. For future designs, John envisions water environments through which human observers may pass inside via plexiglass tunnels. These will afford scientists and visitors remarkable views not unlike the ones John and Anne use in their art.

John and Anne travel extensively to participate in numerous art festivals and gallery showings throughout the United States. The public's heartwarming response has enabled them to expand upon their theme and to embark on even more ambitious projects. The growing recognition of their work furthers their dream of bringing into the world the attitude that we must preserve our living resources. By enjoying this book and responding to the message it conveys, you are participating in that cause.

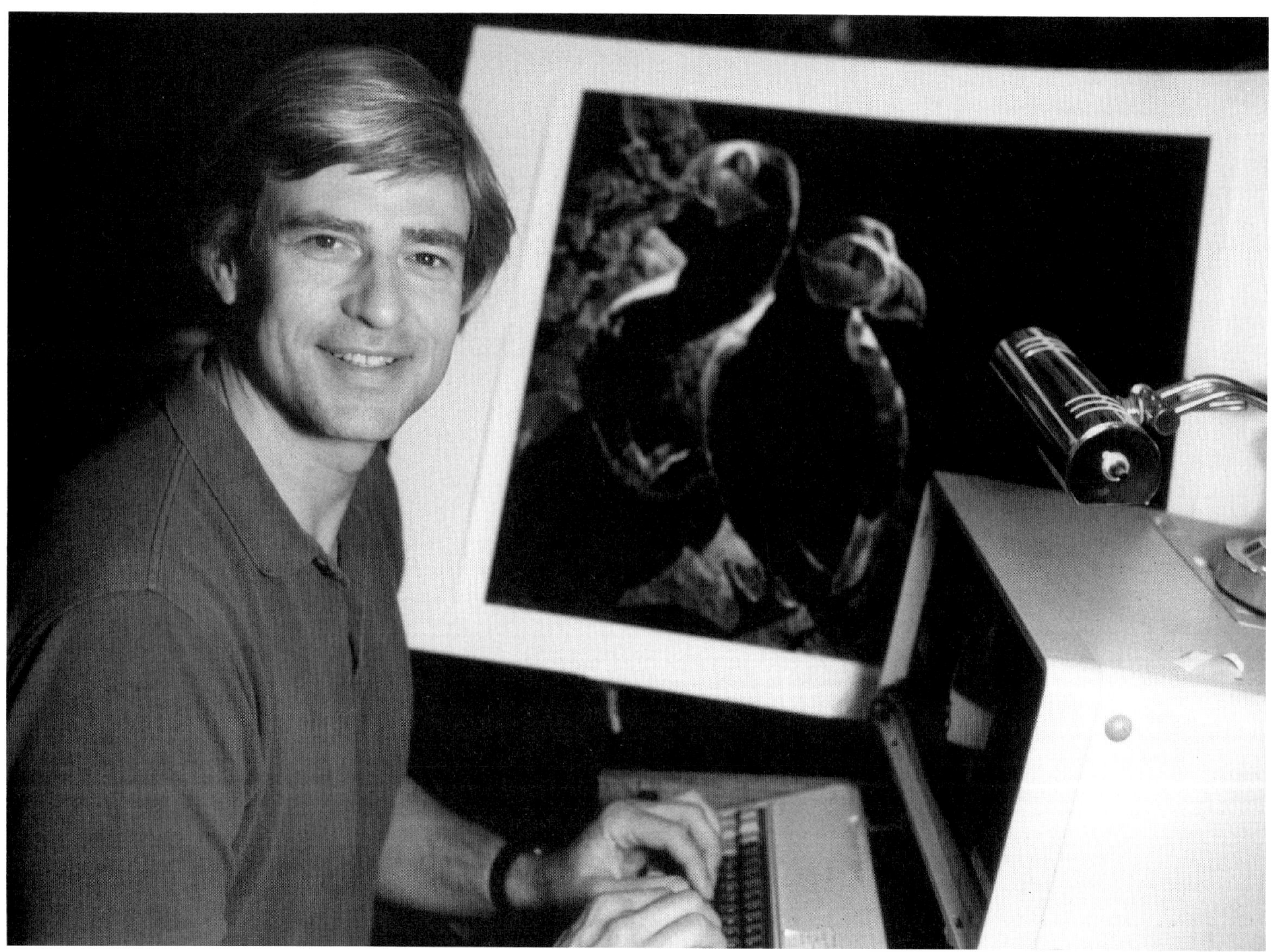

# *About the Author*

Bruce C. Eriksen has a degree in social psychology from the University of California at Los Angeles. He is a published poet and watercolorist, as well as a writer of nonfiction and fiction. He has been a regular contributor and featured poet in *Crosscurrents* literary magazine. He collaborates with his wife, Nancy Chien-Eriksen, at art exhibits throughout the United States, recently producing a book of his poetry and prose and of her art. The book, *Fantasies and Other Realities*, is now in its third printing.

He became acquainted with John Ballou and Anne London's art while participating in various art showings. He was deeply impressed at once by the sophistication and mastery of their art. He was moved by the emotive quality in their naturalistic interpretations of the creatures that he, too, loved. Bruce's longterm interest in marine mammals, wildlife, ecology, and the quality of human existence made it a natural step for him to collaborate with them.

In Bruce's experience as a crisis counselor he had learned that, once the barriers to direct observation such as presuppositions, myths, lack of perspective, and the lack of knowledge are dissolved, fear is replaced by the truth and that a more appropriate peaceful response may emerge. Bruce found that the vision which John and Anne create with their art serves as a wonderful tool which allows the mind to cut through these barriers, like a window, so that one may "see" without prejudice, joyfully.

To capture the spirit of John's and Anne's work, Bruce researched each species' history and behavior at zoos, aquatic parks, natural history museums, and, when possible, in the wild. In many meetings with the artists he grew to understand and feel the spirit and perspective they wished to communicate. Then, studying the artwork intimately, he composed the poetry and prose that comprise the text. It is Bruce's intent to capture the essence of the relationship which John, Anne, and he enjoy with our living natural resources and perhaps to move the readers to experience more closely how miraculously we are all inextricably woven into the fabric of nature.

Bruce lives with his wife and son in Marin County, California, and is at work on another poetry collection, short fiction and nonfiction pieces, and his second novel.

Dear Friends,

In the time it has taken you to read this book, four species have been wiped off the face of our little planet. They were the award winners of sixty million years of evolution, a contest ended by the intervention of our species. Today, as I write, an area the size of New Hampshire was denuded of a forest newly sprouted before dinosaurs were even a possibility.

That loss of territory and its inhabitants is as symbolic as it is real. There is a territory of mind like the rain forests, diminished as much from greed as it is from lack of interest. The nerves that are touched by the howl of a wolf are found on this secret land... the land of our memory generations gone back... a land we cannot surrender to avarice or apathy.

Scenario: When the last zoo closes with the last Asian elephant, a flood of letters will arrive protesting the inevitable. A camera will record the lonely animal's last movements, and a reporter will ask the obvious—why? And on that day the territory of our minds will be diminished... forever.

It doesn't have to happen.

A movement is growing worldwide to stop the march to the brink. It is made up of individuals who still feel the shiver run up their spines when a wolf calls its pack, whose eyes water when their boat is rocked by a curious grey whale, whose hearts pound as the tiger fixes yellow eyes on them at the zoo. Secretly or openly, these people congregate, write letters, donate time—sometimes money—to environmental causes. Their habit started quietly, with the first step usually an inquiry. It is our wish to help you if you are so inclined. On the following page is a list of groups eager to hear your questions.

*Anne London*

# *Starting Points*

You want to do something, but where can you start? The start can be modest: read more and take related classes. You already have an interest. Why not cultivate it? Then, when you have the opportunities, with your friends and community, make your views known—speak out. It is the least you can do.

Better yet, you can join and support a conservation group. As you become more conscious and active you will begin to think with a world view. The ecology of the earth is interconnected.

Refuse to buy animals or plants taken from the wild either illegally or in unclear circumstances. Refuse products made from wild animals, either when on a trip or in your own town. Urging others to boycott these items increases the basic level of conscience and restraint needed worldwide. A healthy, thriving planet is by far the greater reward.

When you can, give of yourself and your own resources. Volunteer at your local zoo, nature center, aquarium, or museum. They have the experience to guide and train you. You see, your contribution can be on a personal level, a community level, or a world level. We have listed below some organizations that would be glad to help you start. You'll be amazed by how much you have in common with them.

American Cetacean Society,
PO Box 4416
San Pedro, CA 90731

American Committee for International Conservation
1601 Connecticut Ave. NW
Washington, DC 20009

American Conservation Association
30 Rockefeller Plaza
New York, NY 10020

American Wilderness Alliance
4260 East Evans
Denver, CO 80222

Center for Environmental Education
1925 K Street
Washington, DC 20036

Cousteau Society
930 W. 21st Street
Norfolk, Virginia 23517

Defenders of Wildlife
1244 19th Street NW
Washington, DC 20036

Ducks Unlimited
PO Box 66300
Chicago, IL 60666

Friends of the Animals
11 West 60th Street
New York, NY 10023

Friends of the Earth
1045 San Some
San Francisco, CA 94111

Fund for Animals
140 West 60th Street
New York, NY 10019

Greenpeace
1611 Connecticut Avenue NW
Washington, DC 20009

Humane Society of the United States
2100 L Street NW
Washington, DC 20037

International Association of Fish & Wildlife Agencies
1412 16th St. NW
Washington, DC 20036

International Society for Protection of Animals
29 Perkins Street
Boston, MA 02130

National Coalition for Marine Conservation
PO Box 23298
Savannah, GA 31403

National Parks and Conservation Association
1701 18th St. N.W.
Washington, DC 20009

National Wildlife Federation
1412 16th Street NW
Washington, DC 20036

Nature Conservancy
1800 North Kent Street
Arlington, VA 22209

North American Wildlife Foundation
709 Wire Building
Washington, DC 20005

Oceanic Society
Magee Avenue
Stamford, CT 06902

Sierra Club
530 Bush Street
San Francisco, CA 94108

Wetlands for Wildlife
39710 Mary Lane
Oconomowoc, WI 53066

Whale Center
3929 Piedmont Avenue
Oakland, CA 94617

Wilderness Society
1901 Pennsylvania Ave. NW
Washington, DC

Wildlife Preservation Trust International
34th Street and Girard Ave.
Philadelphia, PA 19104

Wildlife Society
7101 Wisconsin Avenue NW
Washington, DC 20014

World Wildlife Fund—U.S.
1255 23rd Street NW
Washington, DC 20037

For further information about
Anne London and John Ballou prints,
originals, and books, or other works
by Bruce C. Eriksen, write to:

Wind Dance Publications
113 Rice Lane
Larkspur, CA 94939

or

The London & Ballou Studios
1109 W. K Street
Benicia, CA 94510

# *Artwork Specifications*

|  |  |
|---|---|
| Joie De Vivre *(bottlenosed dolphins)* 3 pieces | 24" x 36" |
| Prelude *(bottlenosed dolphins)* | 20" x 24" |
| Terry and Panama *(bottlenosed dolphins)* | 20" x 24" |
| Ice Caverns *(harp seals)* | 20" x 24" |
| Flukes *(right whale)* | 20" x 24" |
| Long Shadows *(arctic wolves)* | 20" x 24" |
| The Wolf and the Raven | 12" x 20" |
| The Lesson *(sea otters)* | 20" x 24" |
| Orcas by Night | 20" x 24" |
| Shimmering Waters *(orcas)* 3 pieces | 20" x 24" |
| Embrace *(belugas)* | 20" x 24" |
| The Tracker *(bobcat)* | 20" x 24" |
| Walrus Hunt | 20" x 24" |
| African Pelicans | 20" x 24" |
| Humpback and Calf | 20" x 24" |
| Rising *(humpback whale)* | 20" x 24" |
| Like a Dream *(humpback whale)* | 12" x 20" |
| Metamorphosis *(narwhal)* | 20" x 24" |
| Puffins | 20" x 24" |
| Trumpeter Swan and Cygnets | 12" x 20" |
| Serengeti *(leopard)* | 20" x 24" |
| Manatees and Mermaids | 12" x 20" |
| On The Wind *(polar bear)* | 12" x 20" |
| Polar Bear and Cubs | 12" x 20" |
| The One Who Flies *(polar bear)* | 30" x 40" |
| The Arctic Fox | 12" x 20" |
| Silverback and Baby *(gorilla)* | 12" x 20" |
| Penguins | 12" x 20" |
| Making Thunder *(golden eagle)* | 20" x 24" |
| Tiger Lilies | 12" x 20" |
| The Bathing Elephant | 12" x 20" |